In Praise of Gerry Sandusky and *Forgotten Sundays:*

"William Faulkner said, 'The poet's voice need not merely be the record of man. It can be one of the pillars to help him endure and prevail.' This book by Gerry Sandusky is a piece of poetry, a beautifully told story about what makes the game of football in modern America the essence of a man's life—the twin pillars of faith and family."

—Sal Paolantonio, national correspondent for ESPN
and author of *How Football Explains America*

"True inspiration is in short supply in today's football world. Real-life inspiration, I mean. The father-son story of the Sanduskys is one of those stories. It is not always tidy, and not always the kind of good-news story that travels a straight path toward inspiration. There are disappointments, some of them crushing, along the way. But we all can learn a lesson from the way Gerry Sandusky coped with and learned from his father a generation ago, and how he does so today. It's not just a football book. It's a life book."

—Peter king, editor-in-chief of
"The Monday Morning Quarterback"

"John Sandusky was more than a coach—he was a role model who showed everyone around him how to balance professional and personal responsibilities. Even though he wasn't my position coach, Coach Sandusky taught me a lot about the game of football and what it meant to be a player in the NFL. His dedication, worth ethic, and passion for the game rubbed off on anyone who was fortunate to be around him. And he was a friend who always emphasized the importance of family—what it meant to be a husband and a father. Those twin loves—football and family—are described in eloquent detail by his son, Gerry, in *Forgotten Sundays*, a loving portrait of a great coach and a great man."

—Dan Marino, former Miami Dolphins quarterback,
NFL Hall of Fame member

"I was a player for the Miami Dolphins during the trials and tribulations described in the book. Well written with a lot of thought and love. You don't have to play football to feel the impact of this book. This will inspire you to think long and hard about the value of a name and how men communicate life's important lessons to each other—frequently without saying a word."

—**Don Strock, former Miami Dolphins quarterback**

"A father gives you much more than a name. He gives you pride, honor, and love. This is the story of how a son refused to let all that be taken from him, no matter the price."

—**Rick Reilly, ESPN commentator and essayist**

"An excellent account of the emotional rollercoaster of the NFL and the impact this has on families."

—**Larry Csonka, former Miami Dolphins running back, NFL Hall of Fame member**

"Whether it's for the entertaining flashback to the NFL and how the game looked and felt to those of us who grew up watching it in the late '60s and '70s, or the heartwarming remembrance of the father-son relationship that is at the heart of *Forgotten Sundays*, Gerry Sandusky's touching memoir of family, football, and life's passage of time is a gift of a book."

—**Don Banks, *Sports Illustrated* NFL senior writer**

"Gerry Sandusky has truly lived the football life. *Forgotten Sundays* is a poignant look at growing up in the NFL and what family meant to him."

—**Fred Gaudelli, producer, NBC's *Sunday Night Football***

"This is a powerful story filled with emotion and insight about a father, a son, and football."

—**Roger Goodell, NFL commissioner**

"If you've ever had a coach, a mentor, a teacher who helped you become something special, then you understand John Sandusky. He didn't seek the spotlight. He helped others shine. This book provides a unique insight into how John played a key role in our success, but even more importantly it shows from a personal perspective how he was able to stand up to pain and loss without losing character or integrity. It paints a picture of a great coach and a great family man."

> **—Bob Griese, former Miami Dolphins quarterback,**
> **NFL Hall of Fame member**

"Gerry Sandusky captures your attention from the very first sentence. This is a rare, in depth look at a life spent in and around the NFL that few will ever experience. If you love football, you will truly enjoy this emotional, real-life story that everyone can relate to. A must read."

> **—Sean Landeta, former New York Giants and**
> **Philadelphia Eagles punter**

"Forgotten Sundays has the distinct flavor of a great football book . . . however, it's about so much more . . . it's about family, it's about growing up, and it's about a very special father-son relationship . . . "

> **—Mike Mayock, color analyst, NBC and NFL Network**

"My father meant the world to me and taught me so much about baseball and life. It was heartwarming to read the story of Gerry and his Dad in this wonderful book."

> **—Brooks Robinson, Baseball Hall of Fame member**

"Inside a sport so clearly measured by lines, scores, and time, *Forgotten Sundays* takes readers into a world not often explored in football, a world of relationships. This book delves between the games that define careers and explores the relationships that shape lives, transcend generations, and ultimately give strength and value to a name."

> **—Adam Schefter, ESPN Insider**

"A career in professional sports (or coaching if you want) represents a shared sacrifice for an entire family but that sacrifice can also bring families together. In *Forgotten Sundays* Gerry Sandusky perfectly encapsulates and describes that unique dynamic."

> **—Ross Tucker, radio host, color commentator, and host**
> **of "The Ross Tucker Football Podcast"**

FORGOTTEN SUNDAYS

FORGOTTEN SUNDAYS

A Son's Story of Life, Loss, and Love
from the Sidelines of the NFL

by Gerry Sandusky
Foreword by John Harbaugh

RUNNING PRESS
PHILADELPHIA · LONDON

Books published by Running Press are available at special discounts for
bulk purchases in the United States by corporations, institutions, and other
organizations. For more information, please contact the Special Markets
Department at the Perseus Books Group, 2300 Chestnut Street, Suite 200,
Philadelphia, PA 19103, or call (800) 810-4145, ext. 5000, or e-mail
special.markets@perseusbooks.com.

ISBN 978-0-7624-5248-4
Library of Congress Control Number: 2014930071

E-book ISBN 978-0-7624-5249-1

9   8   7   6   5   4   3   2   1
Digit on the right indicates the number of this printing

Cover and interior design by Bill Jones
Typography: Minion and Neutra Text

Running Press Book Publishers
2300 Chestnut Street
Philadelphia, PA 19103-4371

Visit us on the web!
www.runningpress.com

To Lee Ann,
Your love and belief in me makes me a better man.

CONTENTS

FOREWORD
by John Harbaugh

Like me, my friend Gerry Sandusky grew up in a close-knit football family. His father, John Sandusky, was a longtime assistant coach to Don Shula, former head coach, NFL player, and family man. In *Forgotten Sundays* Gerry highlights the importance of family, relationships, and education that shape who we are, while he also shares insights into the intensity of life in pro football. Gerry focuses on his bond with his father, and everyone will relate to some aspect of the dynamics of both John's and Gerry's families. His tales of the father-child bond take you through periods of worship, disillusionment, vulnerability, tragedy, and friendship—and the nuances of each. This book brought tears and smiles as I was reminded of the importance of family and having each other's backs.

Gerry offers some poignant moments from his experiences that take us into the inner circle of his amazing life:

- The elevator ride Gerry shared with Coach Shula, Johnny Unitas, and his father after the Colts lost to the Jets in Super Bowl III

- Learning about how "Big John" Sandusky showed his tender side by singing to his wife as she lay dying of cancer in a hospital

- Gerry discovering the news of Penn State's Jerry Sandusky's arrest just before he joined a Ravens' flight to Pittsburgh

Gerry used the confusion of his name with this criminal as inspiration to encourage others to embrace their family legacies and cherish those memories. His story of being proud of who you are and where you come from is both touching and admirable. How he and his loving family handled this is worth the read. Gerry Sandusky is proud of his name, who he is, and the family he represents.

As the sons of coaches, Gerry and I share a certain bond. But you don't have to be a coach's son or daughter to enjoy the football stories here. The story of John Sandusky, when he was head coach of the Baltimore Colts and put Unitas into a game against the wishes of the general manager is fascinating. Descriptions of working training camps for his father's teams are fun, plus they give insight into that part of the NFL.

How Gerry handled the death of his big brother Joe is inspirational. Gerry came to realize that football and religion could no longer explain everything in life. He provides important insight into his father's march forward after this tragedy despite tremendous emotional pain and personal struggle. And he shares touching moments he experienced and lessons he learned as he watched his father disappear through the harshness of Alzheimer's until John's death.

Heartfelt, intelligent, humorous at times, tragic at others, *Forgotten Sundays* is worthy of your time. It is a coming-of-age story that explores a father-son relationship, the value of a good name, and an interesting behind-the-scenes look at life in the NFL.

ACKNOWLEDGMENTS

I want to thank my amazing literary agent, Wendy Keller, for helping me shape this work from the borderless realm of dream to the manifested reality of dream come true. You remind me that angels exist. To my editor, Geoffrey Stone, we share the crazy coincidence of first names spelled with G that much of the world seems to think belongs to the domain of the letter J. I am forever grateful for your gentle guidance, powerful insights, and your touch of a master in marrying my ideas to the right words in the right places. To my copy editor, Josephine Mariea, you amaze me with your gifts of precision and consistency. Cisca Schreefel, thank you for guiding me through the production process with the insights of a tour guide. To my children, Katy and Zack, no adequate words exist to express the depth of my love and gratitude for sharing this journey with me and filling me with confidence. To my brothers, Jack and Jim, and my sister, Ruth Ann, thank you for the guide and blessing you have each been to me. To Mom, you taught me the power of love—I hope they have book clubs in heaven. To my dear friend Carol Soly, thank you for when, so many years ago, you convinced me to buy my first computer and dared me to be a writer. And finally, to my dad, who left me with a good name—a gift I aspire to give to my children.

— Chapter One —

THAT'S MY NAME TOO

The smell of chalk dust and pencil erasers rose with my desk lid as I searched for my math book, unaware that when I closed the lid, my life would change forever. A jolt of panic zapped me when I saw Ms. Piasecki, my sixth-grade teacher, towering over me. A tall woman, with the large, rough hands of a carpenter and the square jaw of a prison guard, Ms. Piasecki said, "Gerry," in a short, clipped tone. She raised her right eyebrow and said every sixth grader's most feared words: "The principal wants to see you in her office."

In a Catholic school in the early 1970s, I knew not to question authority. My father had reinforced that with a story he liked to tell about how a nun had hit his brother once at school. My grandmother went to the school and confronted the nun. When the nun admitted she had struck my uncle, my grandmother pulled a thick black leather belt out of her purse and handed it to the nun saying, "Sister, you're a woman of God. Don't hurt your hand. Next time, hit the son of a bitch with the belt." I rose from my desk, my hands trembling, my heart pounding, and I walked down the main hallway, a dark corridor the color of goose eggs with a lingering smell of spoiled milk.

By the time I reached the principal's office I wanted to see the nurse instead. The back of my mouth had the tingling sensation I usually felt just before vomiting. A cold sweat soaked through my white shirt. I wasn't entirely sure whether that was sweat or something else making its way down the inside of my quivering knees.

"Hello, Mr. Sandusky," the school secretary said. Catholic schoolteachers and administrators always called you "mister" just before they made you wish you were never born. "You may go into the principal's office." The principal wore the traditional habit of Catholic nuns: dark blue veil trimmed in white and a blue cassock, a fancy name for something that fell in the spectrum of clothing between a dress and a potato sack.

"Your mother called," the principal said. "She would like you to call home right away. Please, use my phone." She nodded toward a black phone that sat near the edge of her expansive desk.

Now I felt set up.

My mother informed me she had good news and bad news. Of course she did. In a Catholic family good news always came attached to bad news. It started that way in first grade when nuns taught that Jesus has cleared our way into heaven. The bad news was he had to die a horribly painful death to do it. Once I digested that lesson I began to expect adults to soften the joy of good news with equal measures of bad news.

"The Colts fired Coach McCafferty today," my mom said.

That was bad news, but I wondered why I got called to the principal's office to hear that. It struck me as stretching the boundaries of cruelty, even for Catholics, to twist my stomach in knots so I could hear that the Baltimore Colts had fired their head coach.

"But I also have really good news," Mom added. "The Colts made Dad the new head coach." If my mom said anything after that I didn't hear it. My father had been a Colts assistant coach since before I was born. Now he was the head coach. I ran my hand along one wall then the other, the grout and coolness of the tile walls assuring me I was awake. This was real. One thought pinballed with me through the hallway as I made my way back to the classroom: *Damn, I'm a head coach's son*. I don't know which felt better: elevating my status at school to a head coach's son or just savoring using the word *damn* over and over in my thoughts.

By the end of the school day kids I had never seen before walked up to me in the hallway, shook my hand, and congratulated me as though the Colts had made *me* their head coach. I had some ideas for my dad's first press conference.

After school I walked with my brother Joe, an eighth grader, to G. C. Murphy's, a five-and-dime store in the shopping center half a mile from our house, where, in theory, everything cost five or ten cents. We wanted to celebrate the news, and Murphy's carried everything we needed: bubblegum, popcorn, and Slushies, a frozen sugary drink, the forefather of Slurpies.

As I paid my nineteen cents for a tall bag of popcorn, the white-haired man behind the counter turned to say something to a thin woman who stood by the Slushie machine. She wore her hair pulled up on top of her head in a tight ball.

"Did ya hear the Colts changed coaches today?" the white-haired man asked the woman.

"Yeah, fired McCafferty," she said

"They named Sandusky the new head coach," the white-haired man said, nodding his approval.

"He's a damn good coach," she said.

I had never heard people discuss my father in public before. Now they were talking about him like he was the pope. The man behind the counter noticed I was still standing there. "You want something else, son?" he snapped at me.

I wanted to say, "Yeah, that's my dad you're talking about," and let him know how good it felt to be me. But because I lived in perpetual fear of adults, I could do nothing more than stammer, "I'd like a Slushie too, please."

"Go around to the other side of the counter, and she'll get it for you," the man said, nodding to the woman behind the counter.

I reached into my pocket. I had a quarter, just enough for a small Slushie.

The man and woman behind the counter continued to volley opinions about my dad. "Has to do better than McCafferty. Christ, the Colts are one and four," the man said.

The woman turned to me and asked in a tone of voice as severe as her pencil-thin eyebrows: "Grape or Coke flavored?"

"Coke. Large, please." I don't know what made me order the large. I knew I only had enough money for a small. My mind and my mouth suddenly seemed to belong to different people. *Change it. Tell her to make it a small. Change it before she . . .* too late. The woman pulled the lever on the blocky metal Slushie machine, and a stream of partially brown liquid poured into a tall paper cup.

I scanned the store looking for Joe and prayed he had a quarter. The woman finished pouring my Slushie and plunked it on the counter. I fished in my pocket, hoping panic would help me find what I knew wasn't there. Joe was nowhere in sight.

The woman turned her attention back to continue her conversation with her coworker. "Sandusky's a tough son of a bitch. I have seats near the field. You can hear him yell. Jesus, I've seen him chew some guys out. Guarantee you no one tries to take advantage of him. And if they do . . ." Sweat poured down my sides. When the woman figured out I didn't have enough money, I would get in trouble—and on Dad's first day as head coach.

I couldn't breathe.

The woman's voice faded as I walked double-time to the door at the back of the store. I sprinted through the parking lot to the safety of the woods behind the store.

Fifteen minutes later Joe stuck his head out the back door, and I lobbed a rock near him to catch his attention.

"Where have you been?" Joe demanded when he reached the place where I had been lying beneath the shelter of Norfolk pine branches where the parking lot met the woods.

"Hiding."

"From who?"

"The Slushie woman."

Joe looked at me as though I had started speaking in a Martian dialect.

"The lady behind the counter. I didn't have enough money. I couldn't find you. I didn't know what to do. She knew all about Dad. Everything. So I ran back here and hid so I wouldn't get caught stealing. That wouldn't look good now that Dad's famous and everyone knows who he is."

Joe looked confused. "What did you steal?"

That's when I realized I had left the Slushie I hadn't paid for and the popcorn I had paid for on the counter.

"You really are an idiot sometimes," Joe said in a tone of voice that made us both laugh. "Brush off your clothes so we don't have to explain to Mom why you're covered in dirt," he added.

As we wound our way along a narrow dirt trail through the woods, I turned to Joe and said, "It feels really cool that Dad's a head coach, doesn't it?"

Joe broke into a grin and nodded. I could tell he felt the same way—a warm, glowing sensation that started deep inside my chest and radiated to my fingertips and toes, to the corners of my mouth, to every hair of my eyebrows. A measure of magic had come into our lives.

"I am a little worried," I confessed, looking up at my big brother the way a remora fish eyes a shark, grateful for his size and shelter.

"Why?"

"Dad's only been a head coach for part of a day, and I'm not handling the pressure too well."

"That's okay," Joe reassured me, draping his arm across my shoulder. "As long as Dad handles it better than you, we'll be fine."

That night we sat as a family in the living room watching the local newscasts, my older brother Jim turning the dial on the TV frantically, switching every few seconds between stations. Each broadcast had a story about my father becoming the Colts' head coach. They showed film of my dad on the practice field. Then he sat at a table, about the width of a picnic table, a bank of microphones in front of him. Interviews with players and fans followed. In the span of six hours it seemed like everyone in Baltimore knew his name, our name. And everyone seemed excited about it.

Everyone but my father.

Later that night, when I saw the headlights to his car sweep into the driveway, I darted out the front door, pelting him with questions by the time he stepped out from behind the steering wheel of his station wagon: "Do you know you were on the news tonight? Do you feel famous already? Dad, are you going to make a lot of changes on the team?"

My dad, an enormous man who stood six feet tall and weighed more than three hundred pounds, gave me a tired-looking half grin and rubbed the top of my head. His right hand covered my short hair like a wool cap. I continued chirping away as he ambled toward the house. I had expected him to step out of the car singing like he did in church, as loud and deep as a foghorn on the Chesapeake Bay. But he said nothing. A frown creased his lips instead of a smile. His short black hair remained perfectly combed, cut above his ears and his collar, with a straight part on the left, reflecting his time in the military.

I added to my monologue as I darted around him: "I guess I should say congratulations, huh?"

His dark chocolate eyes settled on mine, and he spoke for the first time. "Condolences are more like it."

I stood on our front porch and watched him fill the frame of the door, wondering what exactly condolences were and how everyone knowing your name could possibly be a burden? I wouldn't learn the answer to that question for another forty years.

⌒⋎⌒

November 2011

As I walked through the November chill toward the hangar in a remote corner of BWI airport, two members of the Baltimore Ravens security staff greeted me with a question that, by the end of the day, would make me grateful my father wasn't still alive.

As the Baltimore Ravens radio play-by-play broadcaster, I traveled with the team on the charter flight the day before away games. I checked in at the makeshift security checkpoint, a series of folding tables lined up in a long L formation. Craig Singletary, a former Baltimore city cop with a reputation for pulling pranks, asked me, "Are you related to the Sandusky who got arrested on assault charges?"

I had spoken to my older brother, Jim, on my drive to the airport. If someone in the family had been arrested, Jim would have mentioned it, so I shrugged off the inquiry. Before I could say a word another member of the security team, Mo Moore, also a former cop, added to the line of inquiry with the playful grin of a standup comic: "He's the former Penn State defensive coordinator."

Now I knew it wasn't a relative. Over the years people had occasionally assumed we were related. Understandable. Both Sanduskys. Both in football. Both first names sounded identical.

Craig and Mo stared at me with an awkward gaze I would become familiar with over the next eighteen months—eyebrows raised, lips poised at the front end of the word *is*, ready to ask, "Is that your father?" until a pregnant pause swallowed the question, leaving only a silent exchange.

"Not related," I said. I knew of Jerry Sandusky by reputation as a college football coach. I had interviewed him once in December of 1987 prior to a Fiesta Bowl between Penn State and Miami when I worked at a South Florida TV station. "Strange coincidence," I added, "but no relation."

On board the plane I sensed stares as I walked to my seat. I felt them more than saw them, catching only the tail end of stale glances. Each person I passed darted his attention back to his magazine or iPad to avoid eye contact with me, to avoid a visual whiff of something repulsive.

Three or four people sitting nearby asked me the same question Craig and Mo had asked. And before they finished I volleyed back, "No relation." Interest in the topic sparked, spreading a brush fire in every direction, with one whispered sentence igniting another. As soon as I extinguished one inquiry, another lit, followed by another, then another. By the time the plane took off I sensed that every whisper, every visual dagger was aimed toward row 37, seat C—my seat.

Midway through the short flight to Pittsburgh, Colin Ward, our broadcast director, who sat across the aisle to my left, pulled up the story on the Internet and leaned toward me. He said with the gentleness of a funeral director, "This is a lot worse than just assault. He's accused of raping boys."

My stomach landed much harder than the plane.

In my hotel room I watched the local news coverage of the former Joe Paterno assistant being led from his house in handcuffs. Over and over I heard his name. It sounded exactly like mine. Phonetically there is no difference between Jerry Sandusky and Gerry Sandusky.

I ate dinner alone in the hotel bar watching trainers, equipment staff, and assistant coaches on the Ravens staff walk around and away from me rather than pass my table at the risk of making small talk. By the time my plate of rigatoni in vodka sauce arrived, I felt like an animal on display in a zoo: Over here, children, we have a rare example of a Gerry Sandusky. He has the same name as an accused child molester, and we're not entirely sure whether he's related. According to some people, Jerry Sandusky is his father, maybe his uncle. We caution everyone to keep a safe distance because we don't know how dangerous he might be.

The next evening at Heinz Field, where the Pittsburgh Steelers play, I walked onto the field two hours before kickoff to interview Ravens head coach John Harbaugh. The producer of NBC's *Sunday Night Football* broadcast, Fred Gaudelli, a professional acquaintance, walked through the invisible barrier that seemed to keep others a minimum of twenty yards away from me. Gaudelli wore jeans and a sweater. He had the fashionably rumpled look of a Hollywood movie director, his hair slightly too long, only casually acquainted with a comb. "Wow, have I been thinking of you today," he said with the first smile I had seen pointed in my direction in the past thirty hours. "Are people clobbering you over this?" he asked.

"Killing me with whispers," I responded.

As we continued our conversation, Dick Ebersol, the longtime president of NBC Sports and one of the most powerful people in broadcasting, walked over to say hello to Gaudelli.

Fred graciously asked, "Have you two ever met?"

"I don't believe we have," Ebersol said. A tall man in his late sixties with thinning gray hair, Ebersol had the energy of a man more comfortable on the move than standing still. He worked in the stratosphere of broadcasting, a star maker with the power to elevate broadcasters into national treasures or banish them from national attention. I extended my right hand and introduced myself. "Pleasure to meet you, Mr. Ebersol. I'm Gerry Sandusky."

Ebersol flinched at the sound of my name, jerking his shoulders back, withdrawing his hand as though mine were on fire. He diverted his eyes to a cluster of conversations five yards behind me and mumbled an excuse I didn't hear clearly and didn't have the heart to ask him to repeat as he evacuated from my presence.

I glanced at Fred Gaudelli. He had seen the exchange. A brilliant producer, Gaudelli built his career on an ability to assess a situation with the speed of a camera shutter.

He shook his head and muttered, "Wow," shocked at the size of my dilemma. He knew what I had suspected: my name was damaged—not tarnished or nicked, not diminished or overshadowed. Damaged. I pulled the zipper higher on my coat, fighting off the chill of the Pittsburgh evening and the start of what I began to realize was going to be a very long winter.

I was an instant pariah. Feeling completely alone in a rapidly filling stadium, my thoughts turned to my father and how he had handled misfortune puncturing his name, his hopes for the future, and our family.

❧

The sun sets early in Baltimore in December. While squeezing out the last of the sunlight on the horizon, I played catch with my brother Joe in our backyard. Neither of us wanted to talk about what we both knew as we tested each other's arm strength from opposite sides of the yard. The dead, frozen grass crunched beneath me as I ran to catch Joe's pass, superstitiously linking each catch I made to the number of touchdowns the Colts would score in their next game. This time the next game carried more importance than usual.

The Colts had won four games and lost four since my father had taken over as head coach. For my father to finish the season with a winning record, the Colts had to beat the Dolphins in Miami—something no team had done that season.

Our catch ended in the embers of a winter sunset, a glint of orange on the horizon of a gun-metal gray sky, when Joe's last pass slipped through my hands and fell to the frozen ground, a bad omen for the Colts.

When Sunday afternoon arrived Joe and I stretched out in front of the TV in the living room. Joe was taller, thicker, stronger than me. He had big hands, broad shoulders, wide feet, direct DNA hand-me-downs from Dad. Joe was only two years older than me, but he seemed twice my size. I had a more angular and thin frame, like our mom, who shuttled nervously between the kitchen and the living room. She had long, thin fingers that looked at home wrapped around an artist's paint brush or the wooden cooking spoon she currently held in her right hand. The appetizing aroma of roast beef, carrots, and potatoes followed Mom into the living room each time she checked on the game. Joe and I didn't leave the living room, not even for the temptation of Mom's cooking.

By the end of the game we had all lost our appetites.

The Dolphins beat the Colts 17–0.

After the game we stared silently at the TV. Dad stood in the middle of the field, talking to Dolphins head coach Don Shula, who had both of his hands resting on my dad's shoulders.

"What do you think he's saying?" I asked Joe.

"Nothing that's making Dad feel any better," Joe answered.

The TV cameras caught a glimpse of my dad walking off the field, the same glimpse I had caught on the day he became head coach—his stare distant, his jaw clenched, his walk slow, a man in no hurry to his destination.

Three days later I walked home from school with my friend David Muir, who lived on the far end of our street. A small kid with the sudden movements of a squirrel, David's mouth, arms, and legs moved in explosive bursts, darting here, sprinting there. When he spoke he pushed his words together, merging what should have been a few sentences into one long, cumbersome word: *"Doyathinkthey'llhireyourDadbacknextyear?"*

I paused, deciphering David's blurt: Do ya think they'll hire your Dad back next year?

My father had coached for the Colts since before I was born. How could that change? "Of course," I answered.

"Cool," David responded. "ThinkIcangotopracticewithyouone-daynextseason?" I translated: Think I can go to practice with you one day next season?

"Sure."

"Wannaplaysomecatchlateron?"

Before I could deconstruct his ramble, David added the pauses for me. "Play catch," he said, flashing his hands in front of his face to grab an imaginary pass. "Wanna play?" he added for emphasis. "Later on?"

"I'll call you," I said, peeling off in the direction of my house.

"Heyandanotherthingiftheydohirehimback . . ." David's voice faded before I could figure out what he wanted.

David's probes got me wondering whether I might get to watch a few games from the sideline next season. My brother Jimmy, who was eight years older than me, got to watch a few games from the sideline after Dad became a head coach. Jimmy had proof of his experience too: a photo in *Sports Illustrated*. The picture captured Colts running back Tom Matte in midair, diving over the goal line for a touchdown. Jimmy stood on the sideline at the goal line, wearing his gold high school letterman's jacket, his arms thrust in the air like a referee signaling touchdown. After that edition of *Sports Illustrated* came out Jimmy made a show of moving like a peacock around the house in long, dramatic strides, his chest puffed, preening in front of every mirror. You would have thought he had scored the touchdown.

Dad didn't seem as excited.

The morning after that edition of *Sports Illustrated* came out, Dad grumbled at the breakfast table about his boss, Colts general manager Joe Thomas, giving him "a lot of crap" about the photograph. Jimmy wasn't supposed to be on the field, and certainly not that part of the field.

"Tell Joe Thomas to lighten up," Jimmy said. He flashed Dad a smile and ran a hand across the front of his carefully combed hair. "How 'bout I autograph a copy for him?" Jimmy added. Dad returned a stare with the brawn and focused direction of an approaching train that ended the conversation.

We ate quietly and quickly after that. Jimmy had burrowed under Dad's skin. We all knew the warning signs. Dad stared straight ahead. His jaw clicked as he chewed, a metronome of anger. One wrong word now, and Dad might explode through the unstable silence.

When my father smoldered, my brothers, sister, and I all knew to be quiet. Words only compounded the tension. If one of us brought home a D on a report card, we got a stare. If we tried to explain the D, we got an explosive lecture. Once, after losing my bike, I tried to navigate around the mishap during dinner. "I don't know how I lost it, Dad. I laid it on the ground and went to the creek with David Muir. We came back and the bike was gone. I couldn't find it. It wasn't there," I explained, hoping the phrase "It wasn't there" would limit my responsibility and his anger.

Dad glared at me, and when he sensed I had run out of excuses he pointed toward the front door and said, "Go find it. Now." He spoke in short, staccato bursts, four words, each framed by the click of his jaw as he pulverized a piece of roast beef.

Now, as I reached home from my walk with David Muir, I saw Jimmy standing next to the front porch. He had tears in his eyes.

"What's wrong?" I asked. "Get caught in another picture in *Sports Illustrated*?"

"Shut up and go see Mom," he said, tapping his foot against the wooden support beam at the edge of the porch.

I burst through the front door and tossed my denim book bag onto the couch.

"Mom," I shouted toward the kitchen. "Jimmy's crying," I said, eager to learn what had caused my brother's rare show of pain.

Mom stood in front of the stove. The smell of cabbage and ground beef simmering with onions in tomato sauce filled the air. Before I could reach the stove and slip a fork into the stuffed cabbage, Mom put her arms on my shoulders. Her gentle brown eyes beneath puffy eyelids coaxed my attention from the stove. I could see the trail of tears that had moved across her high, round cheekbones.

"Sweetheart," Mom began, "Jimmy's crying because the Colts fired Dad today," she said.

I felt the air fly from my lungs.

I stared at her for a minute, looking for a sign of a practical joke that I knew my mother would never play. All I saw was the sadness and the weight of uncertainty that led each tear across her high cheekbones.

Before long I heard my father's car pull into the driveway. My siblings and I assembled behind Mom at the front door. Joe and I stood behind her to the right. Jack, Jim, and my sister, Ruth Ann, stood to her left, each perched on a higher step of the staircase, a holiday photo waiting to happen, a Christmas card we would never send.

A light snow framed my father as he walked toward the house. Dad carried a blue vinyl zippered pouch the size of a legal pad with a Colts logo in the corner. His breath rose in a frosty trail and drifted behind him, steam off an idling locomotive.

Dad walked in the front door, and Mom wrapped her arms around his thick neck without saying a word.

The rest of us stood rigid, suddenly feeling lost in our own home.

Dad lumbered toward the hallway that led to my parents' bedroom. He paused for a second, glanced down at his Colts pouch, then up at me.

"I don't think I'll need this anymore," he said, handing it to me.

He ran his big hand through my hair and pulled me into the side of his barrel chest. He had an end-of-the-day, musty smell of moldering leaves, the smell of exhaustion and defeat. I felt Ruth Ann hug him from the other side and whisper, "I love you, Daddy."

"I love you too," Dad said in a voice as soft as the falling snow, softer than I had ever heard him speak before. He clipped the end of the last word, his voice cracking. I felt Joe's arms join Ruth Ann's and mine against dad. We clutched him like scared kids holding a tree in a windstorm.

Dad puffed his cheeks and released a long, slow stream of air. The hopes of him ever finding another job, another home, another town, another team that meant as much as Baltimore and the Colts slipped away from me as he exhaled.

A thin rim of red surrounded his eyes as he released us and lumbered toward his bedroom. I walked to the front door stared out at the cloudless December night sky that had followed the snowfall, feeling the sensation of falling into the darkness.

The next day when I came home from school, I heard my father pounding a hammer in the basement. I was surprised to find him hammering nails into two-by-fours in an unfinished corner of the basement. He greeted me with a big grin, a little too big I thought, but better than the disappointment painted on his face the day before.

"Hey there, buddy. Would you hand me that can filled with nails?" he asked, nodding in the direction of his workbench on the far side of the room. I did, and he took a nail and hammered it into place, securing the two-by-four. "There," he said, "good as new."

I didn't know whether he meant the two-by-four or himself. I quietly helped him clean up, picking up his hammer, which seconds before looked no heavier than a dinner spoon in the grip of his hand but felt more like an anvil in mine. As I turned back from the workbench I watched my father move through the basement, his powerful neck set firmly to the task of clearing a path and moving forward. A flush of color had returned to his face, a shade of brick replacing the color of mortar I had seen the day before.

"I guess we'll be getting ready to move soon," I said, hoping my father would assure me everything would be fine.

He bent over and hoisted a wooden trunk from the concrete floor. "We already are," he said.

I swallowed back the tinny taste of fear and uncertainty that rose in my throat.

— Chapter Two —

CONFESSIONS TO MY BROTHER

October 2005

A care nurse greeted me with a smile as I walked into the foyer of the assisted living home where my father now lived and where, each visit, a shock awaited me as I braced to find what Alzheimer's had now stripped from my father's memory. This time what he remembered stunned me.

Dad had moved into assisted living a few months earlier, a move that had accelerated his decline. Jim and I had flown in from Baltimore. We said little to each other on the ride from the airport, letting the warm, moist Florida air pour through the open windows of our rental car, a welcome respite from the chill of early fall in the northeast. We knew Dad's memory of our visit would escape him by the time we put on coats again.

A nurse greeted us at the front desk. She had short brown hair and toned arms, the kind you could see perched over the handle bars of a bike on a ten-mile ride to and from work every day. She had a firm handshake, and as she walked us to Dad's room, leading us down an antiseptic breezeway, she walked with long, fast strides, the only person in sight in a hurry to go anywhere.

A woman with wiry gray hair shuffled by on her aluminum walker and offered a warm greeting. A disheveled-looking bald man clutched an uncombed patch of salt-and-pepper hair on the side of his head as he meandered by us, fully engaged in a loud argument with himself over the colors red and blue.

We walked past a sign marked "Activities Room" in bold white letters and stopped to peer in a door that opened on a half-dozen residents sitting on metal folding chairs, moving their arms and legs in what looked like random spasms. A large African American woman with a smile that filled the room led what the nurse informed us was their most popular exercise class.

Dad had a small, narrow room off a rectangular garden lined by palm trees in the back of the facility. Much of the day he spent sitting in a plastic chair outside the door to his room, staring at the twenty-yard-wide swath of Bermuda grass that separated one side of the courtyard from the other, the way Alzheimer's now separated him from most of the life he had lived.

The bright afternoon sunshine left me unprepared for the plunge into darkness in my father's room. "He doesn't like his room very bright," the care nurse said defensively, preempting any questions about why our father's room had the ambiance of a dungeon.

I knew from our last trip to expect Dad to struggle with our sudden appearance. We had no way to prepare him for our arrival. His room didn't have a phone. The ringing confused him. If we called and asked a nurse to relay a message to him, by the time she left his room the message dissolved in the mist of his vanishing faculties. When we had visited three months earlier Dad just glanced at Jim and me, the same disengaged way he looked at the stack of Robert Ludlum novels on his nightstand. He occasionally joined our conversation in spurts, but his mind had the randomness of a failing computer shortly before it crashes, working fine for a few minutes, then pulling up random files, then nothing at all.

Today Dad sat on the edge of his bed, his hair tousled, in need of a comb, his blank stare aimed in the direction of the beige stucco wall opposite his bed. He had lost his way in the sliver of time between waking from a nap and putting his feet on the floor.

"John," the nurse said, nudging him from his fog. "You have visitors."

Dad turned his attention to Jim and me and said something that struck us with the force of a meteorite slamming into the ground in front of us. He looked directly at me and said, "Joe? Joe? Joe?" His dull, glassy eyes snapped into focus. His slouched shoulders pulled back and squared. I could see for an instant the military training he had received seven decades earlier. "My God, I have missed you. Sit, sit," he said, patting next to him on the bed. "Oh Joe," he said, letting out a long sigh, a sigh he had hidden deep inside of him for the last third of his life.

Jim and I glanced at each other, uncertain what to do, afraid of ruining my father's long-awaited rapture.

Joe had died twenty-six years ago.

❧

At the start of the fall in 1978, my father had begun his third season coaching the offensive line for the Miami Dolphins, and my brother Joe had begun his second season on a football scholarship at Tulsa University. When I had dropped Joe off at the airport a month earlier he slipped a $20 bill in my hand and told me to spend it on a pretty girl, just as a traffic cop barked at me to move my car or else get a ticket.

"Go, get out of here," Joe said. The thought of bringing a ticket home to our father panicked both of us.

As I pulled away from the curb on the upper level of the Fort Lauderdale airport, I glanced in the rearview mirror and saw Joe's broad shoulders passing through the door to the terminal. Something scratched at my thoughts, a subconscious whisper that I had forgotten something, something important. The sensation slipped to my belly with the weight of a sandbag as I realized I didn't say goodbye or I love you to Joe, an oversight I would regret for the rest of my life.

The following month, at midday on a Tuesday, the assistant principal at my high school, Mr. Arculeo, pulled me out of my accounting class and told me my father wanted me to go home immediately. It had something to do with Joe.

My father had never called my school. Never. I knew something was terribly wrong. Mr. Arculeo insisted he drive me home. I insisted he stop at the end of my street so I could walk for a minute and gather my thoughts, which felt as disorganized as plastic green houses and red hotels from a Monopoly game shaken together with Community Chest cards and orange, beige, blue, green, yellow, pink, and white dollar bills then dropped to the ground and spilled from the box.

As I walked down our street, a straight road lined with one-story ranch-style houses, perspiration streamed down my back while a slow, spiraling, contraction rose through my chest.

In my mind I could see Joe gripping the steering wheel of our parents' white Plymouth Duster three years earlier on our move to South Florida as we drove south on I-95. Dad had let Joe give him a break from behind the wheel. It was Joe's passage into adulthood, and we all knew it.

"Don't get too close to the sides of the bridge," Dad snapped. "Jesus, watch the lines on the road, not the goddamn bridge wall. You almost drove us into the wall."

"He's doing fine, John," Mom said calmly from the backseat.

Dad leaned over, pointing at the dashboard, his left index finger tapping the glass in front of the speedometer. "I'll tell you a little trick," he added, lowering his voice to share a secret. "Don't go more than nine miles over the speed limit on a highway, and the cops will leave you alone." He implied that he would too.

The monotonous miles of I-95 rolled by, and after a while Dad closed his eyes, rested his head against the passenger window, and began to snore, a quake that grew from deep in his throat, as loud as the tractor-trailers that passed us. In that moment our family changed. Joe had won Dad's confidence. Even if Joe's thick brown hair was a little longer than Dad thought it should be, he had become a man in Dad's eyes, a man Dad could trust. Our family had no higher honor.

Now I stood at our front door, a threshold I sensed I shouldn't cross. Something had happened to Joe, something awful. Dad wouldn't summon me from school to tell me Joe won player of the week honors in Tulsa's win over Kansas State.

Inside, a dark stillness filled the house. My mom had pulled the drapes in the living room to block the heat of the midday sun. I heard my dad's voice coming from my parents' bedroom in the back of the house. I found him sitting on the side of their bed, finishing a phone call. He wore a white cotton T-shirt with a Miami Dolphins logo on the front and teal polyester shorts with an elastic waistband. He wore white Adidas shoes, the kind with molded black plastic cleats on the bottom to give players and coaches more traction on a field. He had left the practice field to come home.

My mom stood at the foot of the bed tossing clothes into a suitcase with the speed and randomness of a game show contestant trying to beat a countdown clock. She wore her hair tucked back behind a bright red bandana. A wisp of hair fell across her forehead.

When she realized I had entered the room, Mom ran over to me and wrapped her arms around my neck.

"I'm sorry I couldn't pick you up at school," Dad said. Then words escaped him as he struggled to say more. Finally, he found a starting place for an explanation.

"Joe's in the hospital," he spat out.

Mom spoke for the first time. "Something's wrong. Something with his heart. They lost his heartbeat in the ambulance, but, and, uh . . ." Mom's voice trailed off into tears.

The three of us had talked to Joe on the phone the night before. Joe thought he had broken his ribs in Saturday's game. He had sounded shallow, reedy, far different from the bright smile that usually filled his voice, a voice that always sounded excited about football and girls and college. He was scheduled for X-rays today.

"Joe woke up in pain this morning. Had trouble breathing," Dad blurted out. "Mom and I are flying out there in an hour." Then his oversight struck him. "Buddy, I didn't get you a ticket. Damn it. I just called the travel agent. I didn't . . . I wasn't . . ."

"It's okay, Dad," I said, handing him a pair of black socks that had tumbled from his suitcase. Our eyes met, and he nodded his appreciation. He didn't need guilt compounding fear.

Dad sketched a few more details as he continued packing. "Joe's roommate called the trainer . . . hand me my black shoes . . . they called an ambulance . . . grab my Dolphins jacket, no, never mind, it won't be cold there . . . they're having trouble stabilizing him . . . Christ," Dad paused. "They're not even sure what's wrong." Dad shoved the lid of his suitcase closed and clicked the latch. The sleeve of a white shirt spilled from the side.

Then the phone rang.

Mom and Dad reached for it, their hands landing on the phone at the same time, their eyes locked in negotiation. Dad pulled the phone to his ear and angled it so Mom could hear.

"Yes, yes, this is Mr. Sandusky."

"It's the hospital," Mom whispered to me.

"What? I'm sorry. I can't hear you." Dad said, his eyebrows pulled close together, a look that let Mom know he no longer wanted to share the phone.

"I'll take it in the kitchen," she said, running from the bedroom.

"Yes, yes, this is John Sandusky," he said again. Then he listened. After a few seconds he added, "I don't understand. Is my son okay?"

Then he grew quiet and time disappeared.

Silence swallowed us, a dark, plunging silence, too deep to ever fully escape, a gulf that would forever separate the before from the after.

"Doctor, what are you saying? What are you saying?" Dad's words spit into the phone.

I stood still, afraid to move, the way you watch a football game in the final seconds with the score tied and superstition tricking you into believing if you don't flinch you can influence the outcome.

"Is he dead, doctor? Is he dead?" my father asked, his voice rising, an inflection, a plea, a shout. Then his voice crashed along with the phone. "No, no, no."

My father slumped over, his right hand gripping the headboard, the phone a still life on the floor.

A piercing scream broke through the haze.

I ran to the kitchen and saw my mom sliding down the bright yellow wall that the phone hung on, her face the color of cold ashes, the phone dangling like a noose beside her.

"My Joe, no, my Joe, no, no, no." Her chest and shoulders lurched with each sob as I held her, feeling the wetness of her cheeks, her sobs ebbing then rising in piercing shrieks, primal calls of pain.

❧

Now, twenty-six years later, I stood frozen beside my father, watching tears stream down his face, weaving through the stubble of his two-day beard. Jim and I remained silent, careful not to intrude on Dad's reunion with Joe. Instead, it was a loud knock on the door that snatched him from his mirage. An African American woman dressed in medical scrubs let us know the afternoon snack was being served in the dining hall. When I returned to my father's bedside he looked at me, then Jimmy, and said, "Hey, when did you guys get here?" He was smiling, already a safe distance from painful memories.

Much like three decades earlier, my father didn't bring Joe's name up in conversation again. This time, he brought up little more than shards of memories as the three of us sat around a table in the assisted living facility's dining room. A staff member refilled Dad's iced tea and asked if we were his children. He responded not in words or even syllables, just sounds, whispers of consonants. "rrrr" and "cccc." Then he returned his puzzled attention to his half-eaten grilled cheese.

After lunch the three of us made our way to a sun-filled visitors' room with a sofa, chairs, and a large-screen TV. The short walk took nearly as long as lunch. Dad moved in inches now. He carefully lifted his aluminum walker, leaned forward, lowered the walker's rubber-capped legs, and shuffled his feet a few inches. Lift, lean, lower, shuffle. Repeat. The cadence of an old man.

We watched TV, clicking through channels, the previous night's NBA highlights, a gardening show, cooking show, a black-and-white movie starring Jimmy Cagney, and suddenly Dad was totally present as though we had found the right channel to his thoughts with the TV clicker and the gritty voice of Cagney, a movie star in my father's youth.

My father pulled his shoulders back, squaring them beneath his fleshy neck, his brown eyes now clear and focused. "It's really good to see you guys," he said. Dad looked at Jim and shook his head side to side, saying, "I never thought, never for a second thought I would end up like this." He turned his attention to me and continued. "Live your lives now, guys. Don't wait," he said in a crisp, nonnegotiable tone, the one he had used years before when he stood above my bed in the early hours of a Sunday morning, telling me to get ready for church. "It's not fun in the end," he added. "And it all goes by too fast, too fast, too . . ." His voice faded, and like a horizon slipping behind a gauzy, evening mist, his clarity vanished. He was still there, but also gone, more difficult to reach than after we had buried Joe.

❧

Two weeks after Joe died the Dolphins gave my dad the game ball following a 24–10 win over the St. Louis Cardinals. In the long, narrow locker room the players gathered loosely in a circle around quarterback Bob Griese. I stood behind the players and listened.

Griese held a football over his head, the spoils of a Sunday win. He said in a quiet tone, "We all know someone in this locker room has had to fight through the toughest time in his life the past couple of weeks, but through it all he's been here with us, and today his offensive line kicked the hell out of the Cardinals defensive line. Today's game ball goes to John Sandusky."

The players whooped and hollered, as my dad walked into the middle of the circle. His eyes darted between the floor and the players in front of him. His voice had an unfamiliar quiver.

"I know there's a young man in heaven looking down on us right now, and he's smiling." He tried to say more, camouflaging his emotions behind a forced smile. Unable to go on, he held the ball over his head and nodded. His players understood.

In the parking lot I showed Mom the game ball. She nodded, glancing at it, the corners of her lips turned down. Hardly a fair trade.

On the ride home Dad turned on the radio to hear postgame coverage. One of the announcers mentioned the game ball and praised my dad's dedication to the team and his players despite the pain of his son's death. Mom turned off the radio. An awkward silence carried us home. A win, the measure of success in our lives, now felt no different from a loss.

Two months after Joe died I played the first basketball game of my senior season at Cooper City High School. When the public address announcer introduced me in the starting lineup, I ran to the middle of the court as a hush settled on the gymnasium. I looked to my left at the entrance of the gym and saw my father walking in with his entire offensive line, eight men who weighed three hundred pounds or more, Easter Island moving along the baseline. My father had come to plenty of my games over the years, but he had never brought his players with him.

I scored twenty points in the game, but each time I walked to the free throw line, the stillness of the gym gave my thoughts too much liberty to wander. I bent over and dribbled the ball three times at the free throw line. Whap, whap, whap. As the ball snapped back into my hands, I glanced to my left and saw my dad sitting in the second row. Mike Currant, his left tackle, Larry Little, his left guard, sat next to him. Little leaned forward, resting his elbows on his knees, his eyes wide and fixed on me, his mouth open, lips moving slowing mouthing two words over and over: *Make it. Make it.* He wanted my father to have something to cheer for again, even something small, a free throw, the simplest of shots. All of his players wanted that, something to eclipse, if only for a few minutes, the shadow of tragedy that had consumed our lives. I had missed all six of my free throw attempts in the game up to that point. Now, in the final seconds of the game, trailing by one point, I returned my attention to the rim fifteen feet away. I had two shots. The first hit the back of the rim and bounced back to me. I took a deep breath, tried to clear my mind, avoided looking in the direction of my father and his players again. Whap, whap, whap. I dribbled three times, then stared at the rim. And my focus crumbled. I could see Joe at the airport, walking toward the terminal door, and I felt an urge to scream, "Turn around! Don't go! I can never put this family back together again! I'm not as strong as you!"

I don't remember shooting my second free throw. I only remember seeing it in midair, just as I turned to look at my father and heard the ball clank off the rim. The buzzer sounded, *ERRRRRRRRRR*, signaling the end of the game. The sigh of a missed opportunity rose from the wooden bleachers. My father pursed his lips and lowered his eyes. My father had come to the game to make me feel better, and I had missed a chance to do the same for him.

❧

Now I sat next to my father in the sunny common area of his assisted living facility. An episode of *Murder, She Wrote* had replaced *Cagney &Lacey* on TV. Before long, Dad nodded off and began to snore, a low-vibration hum that signaled the change in direction of his breath. Even the magnitude of his sleep had diminished, stripped of the force he had once wielded during his naps, a snore that years before had sounded like loose bolts vibrating on the bed of a pickup truck.

A commercial came on promoting a DVD set of the Miami Dolphins' greatest games and memorable moments. I didn't need to call the 800 number. I had seen many of those games and lived through the moments, sometimes standing right next to my father all the while feeling far away.

The year after Joe's death I left for college a thousand miles away in Maryland at Towson University, just north of Baltimore. Each trip home I found our house darker, dustier, as though sadness stifled the sunlight. Mom still smelled like her garden, a creamy whiff of gardenia lingering in her hair, the herbal scent of hibiscus, grass, and soil on her hands. But now Joe's grave had become her garden. She visited it every morning, brought fresh flowers, trimmed the grass around his headstone, swept dirt from the raised brass letters that spelled out his name. She frequently slept in Joe's old bedroom, where everything remained as it had been on the day he died. His high school letter jacket still hung in his closet, along with his jeans and the shirts with the western-style yoke Mom had made him on her sewing machine. The chill of a museum had crept into our home.

Dad spent most of his time coaching. At home he would sit in his favorite chair in the living room, a gold-and-brown-flecked upholstered lounge chair with a wooden handle that released a footrest as the top half of the chair reclined. When he pulled on the handle on the left side of his chair, it also usually catapulted him into a nap. Mom would retreat to the kitchen or to her sewing machine to escape his snoring, the soundtrack of her isolation.

Dad had no escape but football. Mom preferred to escape football. It had taken her son's life and her husband's attention.

During my winter break in January of 1982 the Dolphins faced San Diego in Miami's Orange Bowl, a rusting old horseshoe-shaped stadium that could rattle like a tin shack in an earthquake when the crowd grew excited. Joe and I had spent dozens of Sundays there, helping the Dolphins' equipment manager in the locker room and on the field—fixing helmets, tightening cleats, running water bottles onto the field during timeouts. I always felt out of place on the field after Joe died, a sidecar detached from a motorcycle. But I wanted to see my father up close with his players again, especially because some of them were about the age Joe would have been now.

Before the game I joined my father in his pregame ritual, sitting on the team bench, quietly thinking about the game ahead. The lines in his cheeks and neck had become more deeply etched. The fury I remembered in his eyes from my childhood remained, but it was buried far deeper, coal in the belly of the earth. Dad struck me as a man who had moved a thousand miles away from his own life.

By the end of the first quarter, through a series of fumbles, interceptions, and blown plays, the Dolphins had fallen behind 24–0. Then, for the first time in three years, I saw football transport my father again to a place where he looked alive and free of the burden of grief.

The Dolphins had pulled back within two touchdowns. Before the final play of the half, the Dolphins' quarterback, Don Strock, huddled on the sidelines with my father and Dolphins head coach Don Shula. I handed Strock a paper cup filled with water and stepped back while the three men talked.

"We're going to run it now." Shula said to Strock and my father, an affirmation, not a question. "Eighty-seven circle curl lateral." Shula had the presence of a general on a battlefield, his right hand on his hip, his jaw set squared, his will leaning into a challenge.

Strock nodded, and my father, adding to the verbal cipher of a football play call, said, "Remember, run it out of double left to give yourself the best protection . . ."

When they finished, Strock trotted back toward the Dolphins' huddle at midfield. My dad turned toward me and winked. Shula stared at the field, waiting to see whether their plan would catch the Chargers off guard.

Strock threw a fifteen-yard pass near the right hash mark to wide receiver Duriel Harris. The Chargers' defensive backs converged on Harris, but just before they tackled him, Harris flipped the ball at a forty-five-degree angle toward the sideline, and out of nowhere, Dolphins running back Tony Nathan snatched the ball at a full sprint and ran, untouched, for a touchdown as the first half came to an end.

The Orange Bowl erupted. Shula and my father faced each other and pumped their fists in the air, riverboat gamblers who bet on a trick play, the hook and ladder, a play that put the Dolphins back in the game.

Dad jogged by me on the way to the locker room and flashed a huge grin, one I hadn't seen in three years, the kind of smile that began in his eyes, opened his mouth, and revealed his teeth, an involuntary action with the swiftness of an electric current. I wished the game could have ended right then.

In the second half the Dolphins and Chargers traded the lead until a Chargers touchdown in the final minute sent the game into overtime.

I walked along the Dolphins' bench, handing out towels. I brought my father a cup of water as he took a knee in front of his linemen and gave them instructions. His voice rose above the din of screaming fans. "They're shifting pre-snap from an over to an under. Let 'em. Whichever way they shade is where they'll slant." He reached for a whiteboard, wiped the sweat from his forehead with the back of his hand, and diagramed a blocking scheme. "We've got this," he said, brimming with certainty. As he rose from a knee, my father tapped one of his players, Bob Kuechenberg, on the top of his helmet and said, "Where else would you rather be right now?" Football, at least for this day, had become everything again. My father seemed immune to the chaos of the moment, coaches shouting, players running on and off the field, a swirling noise of seventy thousand cheering fans making communication impossible from farther than three feet away. He fit here. He had a place where he could stand up to the storm, a storm he could understand, measure, calculate, and maneuver against. He adjusted his black headset just so and marched back to the sideline.

The Dolphins and Chargers missed scoring opportunities in overtime until San Diego won the game with a field goal, a perfectly kicked ball that sailed through the uprights and ended the game, shattering the illusion that had held my father captive for the previous three hours.

My father peeled off his headset and handed it to an assistant equipment manager. I caught up with him on his walk to the locker room. His season had ended with the thud of a kick. I hurt for my dad, but I had no words to comfort him. After a few shared steps in the direction of the tunnel at the closed end of the stadium leading to the locker room, he put a sweat-soaked arm around my shoulder and said, "Helluva game, huh?" He glanced at me briefly and then looked away, far away, and whispered, "It's okay, pal. We've been through a lot worse."

⌘

Unfortunately life now had no more illusions left for my father, just confusion. When he woke from his nap, he stared at Jim and me with a look of vague recognition.

"Hey, Dad," Jim said, easing him from his confusion. "It's Jim and Gerry. We came by to see you today."

Dad mumbled something and then said more clearly, "You guys came from Baltimore?"

"We did," Jim said.

"Didn't I used to live there?" Dad asked.

"Yes. Yes, you did," I said.

"When was that?" he asked.

"A long time ago, Dad. A long time ago," I said, wishing I could give him a glimpse of the force he once was before loss had robbed him of his future and Alzheimer's had robbed him of his past.

— Chapter Three —

WHEN HEROES FALL

My father's past included a sideline role in one of the most important games ever played in the NFL. History books point to the birth of the National Football League in the 1920s, but football fans will tell you that the NFL really began on the day they saw their first big game. For me that day unfolded in the exotic, tropical warmth of the Orange Bowl in Miami, Florida, on January 12, 1969, the day the Baltimore Colts played the New York Jets in Super Bowl III.

My dad coached the defensive line for the Baltimore Colts. Like a lot of eight-year-olds, I thought I had the best dad in the world. Now, I would have proof—a Super Bowl ring with my father's name on it.

My mom had sent a note to school the previous week to alert teachers that my brother Joe and I would miss a few days of classes to go to the Super Bowl. Every teacher except Mrs. Brown, my English teacher, had asked with an exaggerated grin whether she could come too. Mrs. Brown handed me a stack of papers as she leaned her face close to mine, her hot breath smelling of stale coffee. She added with a sneer that she expected me to hand them in completed the day I returned.

By the time the game arrived I had nearly forgotten about the stomachache I felt every time Mrs. Brown looked at me, her asphalt eyes tucked under a furrowed brow beneath short brown hair that framed her round face like a World War II army helmet.

From our seats in the upper deck of the Orange Bowl, I could see palm trees behind the scoreboard in the open end of the stadium. The skyline of Miami stood in the distance—Oz with coconuts. The thought moved casually across my mind, as easily as the South Florida breeze, that I hadn't done any of the work Mrs. Brown had assigned me. I felt my stomach twist in the grip of worry, but I talked myself past the cold sweat that followed by remembering I didn't return to school for two more days. By then a Colts Super Bowl win would overshadow everything, especially homework. A victory parade would probably buy me an extra day to do the work and avoid Mrs. Brown's volcanic anger—not to mention my father's reaction to the note she would send home from school: *Gerry has received and "F" for failing to do his assigned work.* The Jets didn't worry me; Mrs. Brown did.

Every morning I had set my mind to beginning the homework assignment, but playing in the hotel pool with my brother had an alchemist's effect on time, turning minutes into hours and making them disappear in a sunset that snuck up on me with an evening chill. Just when it seemed certain my mother would direct me back to our room to do homework, my dad would appear, his work day behind him. Joe and I would lure him into the pool, climbing on his massive back like circus clowns riding an elephant. My father would dunk us underwater and shake us off with the ease of a dog shedding water after a bath, then he would swim after us, laughing when he caught us and tossed us in the air like cliff divers into the deep end of the pool.

By the time we got back to our room exhaustion had swallowed me, and my homework would wait for another day.

The Super Bowl had arrived before I filled out a single page of my English assignment. Homonyms and subject-verb agreement could wait. I would lean on my idols in blue football jerseys to win me a grace period from Mrs. Brown. Surely, even she would get caught up in a Colts Super Bowl celebration.

The Colts and Jets jogged onto the field, looking as mismatched as their uniforms. The Colts wore royal blue jerseys with white numbers and shoulder stripes, white pants with blue stripes, and white helmets with a blue stripe down the middle and blue horseshoe emblems on either side. The Jets had all-white uniforms with green stripes and numbers. A green center stripe bisected their white helmets. On either side of the helmet was the green outline of a football with the word Jets written in white over the outlined initials NY. Joe and I had long since agreed that the Colts' uniforms had an elegance to them—classics, the mark of champions—while the Jets looked college, even small college.

A bald man sitting directly in front who had wild tufts of gray hair on either side of his head, where most teams placed the logo on their helmets, jumped to his feet and, in a heavy New York accent, pointed out Jets quarterback Joe Namath to the two boys who sat next to him. They looked like his grandsons. "There he is. Over there," he said. It sounded more like "Dairy iz. Ova dare."

In the game program Namath's photo resembled drawings I had seen in religion books at my elementary school—photos of Satan. Namath lacked the horns of Beelzebub, but they both had large noses, dark eyes, and long hair. The nuns at my school, Immaculate Heart of Mary, often cautioned that Satan could disguise himself to fool people, make himself more popular. He could use money, clothes, and fame to lure people into his grasp. Judging from the reaction of the bald man in front of me and a lot of other people in the Orange Bowl, it occurred to me that Satan had fooled New York.

"There's Dad," I shouted, looking through my binoculars and leaning as close to the man in front of me as I could without touching him. I wanted him to know what a winner looked like. My father was easy to find. He weighed 300 pounds—228 pounds more than me. He wore a white shirt and ran his hand through his thick, short, dark hair. I kept my binoculars glued on him as he walked along the sideline and put on a headset similar to ones pilots wore. He used the headset to talk with other Colts coaches during the game. The headset had one dark, oval earpiece that covered his left ear, a thick black band that stretched across the top of his head and stopped just short of his right ear, which remained uncovered. A flexible black wire about the width of a pencil extended from the earpiece in front of his mouth, with a microphone at the end about the size of a Tootsie Pop. Dad didn't answer me the one time I asked him whether, when he put on his headset, he ever felt the urge to say things like, "Vector, Charlie, Roger, you are cleared for landing on runway seven, bearing five-zero-niner." He just looked at me and shook his head.

Even in a world dominated by large men, my dad stood out. He had a barrel-shaped chest, midnight-black hair, a thick neck that fused with shoulders as broad as a terrace, and a smoldering, brown-eyed stare, all neatly balanced above powerful legs and size-14 shoes. The edges of his lips sloped into a natural scowl, and when he opened his mouth his baritone voice could rattle glass and my confidence. His voice reached inside of me with the force of a cathedral bell, reverberating to a deep place where I kept my dreams and the first sprouts of confidence. My father's voice could yank every sprig in the time it took him to pronounce my name.

A few years earlier he had recruited me to help fix a leak in the water heater in our basement. He stretched out on his back on the concrete floor, positioning himself to reach under the water heater, and I handed him the tools he called for. With each handoff from my small hand to his mammoth one, I felt a little more valuable. Pliers. Screwdriver. Wrench.

He had wedged himself between the water heater and the concrete block wall, no longer able to make eye contact with me. I could only hear his voice and see his left hand. "We've almost got this thing fixed," he said. My pride mushroomed over "we." He wiggled his index finger and asked for a Phillips-head screwdriver. I had no idea what that meant, so I guessed and handed him the largest screwdriver I could find in his toolbox.

"No, a Phillips head," he said, the timbre of his voice starting to unsettle me. I rifled through his toolbox a second time, looking for the word *Phillips* but saw only *Craftsman* on the handle of his screwdrivers. My next guess produced a blast from behind the water heater.

"Damn it, Gerry, a Phillips head!" he barked. The tendril of confidence that had bloomed seconds earlier began to wither. "I'll be right back," I said. Then I ran to the backyard where my mom was working in the garden and asked her what a Phillips head was.

"It's a screwdriver," she said in a gentle voice.

"I don't think so," I said and recruited her help to find the screwdriver.

As she opened the door to the basement, my father, still wedged between the water heater and back wall, was yelling now. "Gerry! Where the hell are you?"

"I've got it, John. Calm down," Mom said, reaching into the toolbox.

Her voice must have surprised my dad, because he banged his head on the water heater, hard, the deep, vibrating sound a baseball bat makes colliding with metal. "Son of a bitch!" he bellowed.

"I don't think I like Phillips heads, Mom," I whispered.

She nodded toward the back door, and I took my cue, slipping out of the basement while my father's voice wrapped itself deep inside my chest and suffocated the bud of accomplishment he had planted there two minutes earlier.

Now, in the seconds leading up to the start of the game, I felt a similar twinge of uneasiness, a knowing at the top of my stomach, the feeling of bad news trying to intrude. I felt helpless and small, sitting in the upper deck of the Orange Bowl, a small point of view in a crowd of seventy thousand people, with no power to influence the game but plenty at stake.

At the opening kickoff a rush of energy pulsed through the crowd. For a second I felt like I might lift off into the brilliant blue sky, a kite with no string. I reached out and clutched my mom's hand. She must have felt the same way because I could feel her long, thin fingers return the neediness of my grip.

The game started ominously for the Colts. Lou Michaels missed a twenty-seven-yard field goal early in the first quarter. Near the end of the quarter, with the Colts in scoring range again, quarterback Earl Morrall's pass deflected off the hand of a Jets defensive lineman, wobbled and hung in the soupy, Florida air before falling into the hands of a Jets defensive back in the end zone. The crowd erupted with the unsettling surprise of glass shattering on a kitchen floor.

"Randy Beverly! Yeah, baby! Randy . . . goddamn . . . Beverly," the old man in front of me shouted.

"It's okay," my mom said. I wasn't sure whether she meant the language the man in front of us used or the Colts' second squandered scoring opportunity. Her reassuring voice, as gentle as the warm Miami breeze, was my refuge of unlimited patience. She used the same tone when I left my backpack at school or left the grass clippers in the yard in a thunderstorm. "It's okay" implied she wouldn't tell dad about it.

But even she couldn't hide a scoreless quarter from my father. The Colts were seventeen-point favorites. I thought they would have blown out the Jets by the start of the second quarter. So did everyone else other than Joe Namath, who had predicted a Jets win, a comment that had caused more than one nun at my school to mention with a finger wag in my direction that pride goeth before the fall. I didn't know why Namath's comments earned me a lecture, but the memory percolated a sour taste of bile in the back of my mouth every time I looked at the green number twelve on his jersey.

My brother Joe looked as uneasy as I felt. Beads of sweat bloomed on his forehead as he stared at the field, his chin resting on the palms of his hands, the warmth of South Florida starting to stagnate. I began to suspect Satan knew how to use weather to his advantage too.

Through my binoculars I could see my father talking with Don Shula, the Colts' head coach. Shula had short, dark hair parted on the side and a stare that could melt a metal door. Just before he yelled at someone Shula's jaw jutted out like the bottom drawer of a dresser. Joe said Coach Shula got mad because he had a lot of job pressure. "Kind of like you feel the night before school if you didn't do your work for Mrs. Brown's class," Joe said. I wished he had used a different example, as the metallic taste of biting aluminum foil rose from the back of my throat, the taste of bad things to come.

Coach Shula turned away from my father, and for an instant he seemed to look in my direction. I quickly lowered my binoculars, feeling a breathless sense of panic, the sensation of an icy hand wrapping around my throat, the feeling I woke to on days I had a test in Mrs. Brown's class.

As time drained from the game clock in the second quarter Namath led the Jets down the field. At the end of the drive Namath handed off the ball to Matt Snell, who ran to his left, lowered his shoulder, and plowed over Colts linebacker Dennis Gaubatz at the goal line, scoring the game's first touchdown.

The Jets fans in front of us leaped from their seats. The old man, now chomping a cigar, turned around to celebrate with someone sitting behind me. For a second I made eye contact with him. The old man grinned, revealing crooked, barley-colored teeth speckled with dark spots as unevenly as stale toast. I wanted more than anything for my father to come up into the stands and wipe the grin off his face the way my father had done the previous summer during one of my baseball games.

My dad had filled in as the umpire for one of my little league games.

The first time I came up to bat my father bent over home plate, brushing it with a whisk broom he had pulled from his back pocket. As he stood up he whispered to me, "Swing at anything close."

The first pitch was outside. He called strike one.

A man in the stands, who had complained earlier in the game about the umpiring, shouted, "Go see the eye doctor across the street after the game, ump."

The second pitch came in low, a little inside. He called it strike two.

"Christ Almighty, do you get anything right, ump?" the man in the stands yelled.

My father peeled off the umpire's mask and walked around the backstop. The smattering of parents in the stands froze. "Get down here. Right now," my father said, pointing a finger at his heckler. The man glanced to his left, then his right. My father added, "You know who I'm talking to. Shall I come up there?" The man had wavy black hair and, as he stood and walked toward my father, he held his hand against an emerging belly. When he reached my father at the bottom of the bleachers the man opened his mouth, but my father cut him off.

"You've said enough today," he emphasized his point, poking his index finger in the man's chest. "I filled in as umpire so these kids could play their game. They don't need to hear your loud mouth. And neither do I."

The man nodded, a strawberry tint of embarrassment coloring his cheeks.

"Say one more thing that doesn't help teach these kids good sportsmanship, and I'm going to stuff your fat little ass in this trashcan," my dad barked before walking back to his position behind home plate. As he pulled his mask back on, he looked at me and winked. On the next pitch he called me out on strikes.

Now, at halftime, I needed my dad to thump his finger into the chest of the bald man with the thick New York accent in front of me. But with the Colts trailing 7–0, I knew my dad had bigger problems to handle.

I looked to Joe to find a reason not to worry. He was two years older than me and nearly twice my size. Like most brothers close in age, we fought a lot, mostly in a simmering war of words that occasionally mushroomed into a wrestling match that I was doomed to lose because of Joe's size. That day alone we had fought over who went first in line at the hotel breakfast buffet, who sat next to the window on the bus ride to the stadium, and who sat closest to the aisle at the Orange Bowl. Joe gave in to my pestering, despite knowing he could get his way with one punch unseen by our mom, a punch he might threaten but would never throw.

Dad had taught Joe to protect me. He let us argue and wrestle but never punch. Joe had a square, chunky frame with big hands and feet as oversized as a mastodon pup. I had narrow shoulders, elbows and knees too large for my thin arms and legs, a ribcage as pronounced as a hungry pigeon. Unfortunately for Joe, I had overheard my father's instructions a few years earlier: "No punching him. You'll hurt him," Dad said. "And that includes even when he deserves to be punched," he added, clenching his right hand in a meaty fist to underscore his seriousness.

I used that to my advantage, knowing I had invisible armor—until I pushed too far.

One Saturday afternoon Joe and I argued while playing football in our backyard, emulating the way NFL Films transformed football into dramatic theater with dramatic, orchestral music, slow-motion footage, and sonorous narration. The argument stemmed from me pretending to run the ball in slow motion while saying in the deepest, most dramatic voice I could manage, "Gayle Sayers sweeps to the left of the vaunted Chicago Bears offensive line."

Joe cut in, saying, "But big number seventy-eight, Bubba Smith, of the Baltimore Colts, stops the electrifying Bears running back with a game-saving tackle." Then he reached out, yanked on my sweatshirt and flung me to the ground, pouncing on the fumble my collision with the frozen soil caused.

As Joe walked away, holding the football over his head, I darted at him and lunged from behind, my skinny right forearm rattling off the back of his head. Then I heard my father's voice belting out from our back porch.

"Oh no you don't," he said.

He had seen everything. Before I could say a word in my defense, Dad nodded toward Joe. His voice had the rumble of close thunder. "Kick his ass and teach him a lesson."

Joe pounced on me, his restrained frustrations unleashed, his punches peppering my head and chest until Dad shouted, "That's enough. And you, you little shit," he said, pointing at me, "you ever cheap-shot your brother again, I won't make him stop so soon."

Before I could whimper, "Yes, sir," Dad walked back into the house.

Joe never had to hit me again.

Now, with the Colts in a situation more precarious and less believable than anything Joe and I could conjure in a backyard football game, my brother put his arm around me and told me not to worry so much. "It's only 7–0," he said. But his words lacked the conviction I had once felt from his punches.

The third quarter began with a disaster. Colts running back Tom Matte fumbled. The Jets recovered. New York extended its lead to 10–0. A few minutes later the Jets added another field goal. 13–0. Joe had stopped reassuring me. Mom put her arms around both of us. None of us dared to look at Dad through the binoculars.

Midway through the third quarter the Colts replaced quarterback Earl Morrall with Johnny Unitas. An injury had kept Unitas from playing for much of the playoffs. Now, as Unitas jogged onto the field, I felt a tug of hope.

Mom, Joe, and I held hands the way we did at church when we prayed for something important, like a speedy recovery for an usher at the seven-thirty mass who had a heart operation, or the pope, or Johnny Unitas. He was Catholic and attended the same church we did, Immaculate Heart of Mary, a long, rectangular building constructed from gray flagstones, capped with a peaked wooden roof decorated on the inside with elaborate gold and red stripes and ornate silver swirls, a design more suited to a papal decree than a church roof in a blue-collar neighborhood. On Sundays Unitas attended the 7:30 mass. We did too. When Unitas stood, I stood. When Unitas kneeled, I kneeled. When Unitas sat, I sat. In school the nuns taught me to follow the priest at mass. I preferred to follow Johnny Unitas.

I went to the same barbershop as Unitas too, a trip I always made with my father, sitting beside him in the front seat of his Vista Cruiser station wagon, quietly hoping to find Unitas in the barber chair when we walked into the shop. Before the barber could ask me how I wanted my hair cut, I would answer, "Same as Johnny U"—a buzz cut on the sides with a flat top.

If anyone could save Super Bowl III, Johnny Unitas could.

In the fourth quarter New York stretched its lead to 16–0. Late in the quarter Unitas led the Colts on a scoring drive, capped by a Jerry Hill touchdown run. Hill, who spelled his first name with a "J," always made a point after Colt practices on Saturday mornings at Memorial Stadium of playfully teasing me in the locker room that I spelled my name wrong: "Who spells Gerry with a G?" I had nothing more than a shrug and grin in return as I helped the equipment manager pick up dirty towels and jerseys from the concrete floor. I had no inkling of how important the difference between J and G would become to me in another four decades. For now the difference between a win and a loss held more significance than two consonants that seemed as closely related as cousins. With only about three minutes left in the game and trailing 16–7, the Colts needed a miracle to win.

My mom sought comfort from a higher source than Johnny Unitas, turning her attention to the mother of Jesus. My mom ran her right index finger and thumb along a circular string of rosary beads as she mumbled a series of Hail Mary's. I suspected a different combination of words involving mothers found their way out of my father's mouth.

A few minutes later, as Unitas's final pass fell incomplete, I learned the mother of Jesus didn't pay nearly as much attention to football as you might expect from a woman who had a pass named after her.

The Colts lost 16–7.

A mob of players and fans surrounded Joe Namath as he ran toward the tunnel leading to the Jets' locker room, his right arm raised, his right index finger extended. I had a different finger in mind.

The old bald man in front of us lit a fresh cigar and began singing . . .

"Start spreadin' the news . . ."

He was celebrating evil.

"I want to be a part of it . . ."

Maybe he did, but I didn't. Mom, Joe, and I didn't say a word.

"New York . . . New York . . ."

I stared at the rivers of people moving around the Colts and Jets players at midfield, blue eddies of agony, green whirlpools of euphoria.

"I wanna wake up in a city . . ." Cigar smoke wrapped around the old man in front of me while a sinking feeling anchored me to the metal bench I sat on.

I scanned the field with my binoculars looking for my father and found him near the end zone, walking off the field, alone. His shoulders sagged, and his gaze fell only on the stretch of grass in front of his strides. He didn't look at what I couldn't miss: Jets fans dancing, jumping and hollering, waving jerseys and banners. The tropical surroundings had fallen into the chaos of a revolution. Green had become the color of celebration, blue a shade of embarrassment. I had seen the Colts lose before, but I had never seen my father look defeated. I glanced up at the scoreboard: Jets 16. Colts 7. Time and hope had expired. There was no next chance, next play, next week. He was already wearing the loss, not like sweaty clothes you peel off and change after a shower but like a birthmark, something permanent you may not have wanted but have to learn to live with. The clench of his jaw made me think my dad needed a much longer walk than the one to the locker room.

The old Jets fan finally left, leaving a trail of cigar smoke behind him, a smelly shroud that stood between my father and me as I watched him disappear into the tunnel.

"I saw Dad," I said to Joe in the hushed tone of an uncomfortable secret.

"How did he look?"

"Like we're going to get yelled at a lot this winter."

A few hours later, back at the team hotel in Fort Lauderdale, I found myself in an elevator with my father, Don Shula, and Johnny Unitas. A day earlier and this intersection of time, place, and people would have felt like the granting of a wish. Three heroes and me, together, alone. But now with the elevator, like so much of that day, slow to move, the closing doors trapped me in smoldering silence. My father, coach Shula, and Johnny Unitas all looked straight ahead, the heavy, uneven breathing of a wounded bear filled the space. As the elevator rose, my tears began to fall. I snuffled them back as much as I could, wiping my eyes with my sleeve. I didn't want to cry in front of the three most important men I knew. But I couldn't help it. How had the Colts—the Colts—lost to the Jets—the goddamn New York Jets? I knew second graders from Catholic school weren't supposed to use that word, even in their thoughts, but my dad always said, "god damn it" when he got mad. It came out with volume that rose like an incoming tide as his baritone moved through the words: god DAMN IT! Three syllables connected with the invisible thread of anger, each syllable louder than the one before it, only the briefest of pauses between them. Sometimes when he was *really* mad Dad stretched out *god*: "goooood DAMN IT." And when his anger morphed into fury, the space between the syllables disappeared, the three bursts of sound rising together into a mushroom cloud of anger: "godDAMN*IT*!"

I didn't dare say it out loud, just to myself. God damn it, goddamn it, goddamnit.

The elevator stopped, and Unitas got off, pausing briefly to rub his hand across the top of my buzz cut and say, "You're not the one who should be crying."

When the elevator door closed behind Unitas, my dad put his thick, heavy arm around my shoulder and pulled me close. I buried my face into his side, wondering whether the elevator would ever get to our floor so I could collapse in my bed and pretend my heroes still remained as perfect and intact as an unopened pack of football trading cards.

Chapter Four

FAREWELL TO HEROES

I saw the goddamnit look frequently in the months after my dad became the Colts' head coach, except for one Sunday in December, the Colts' last home game at Memorial Stadium, the last game I would hear my father introduced as the head coach of the Baltimore Colts.

Wind blew through Memorial stadium, the kind that followed the layout of the stadium, pushing in from the open end by the scoreboard, sweeping along the seats on the Colts sideline, making a 180-degree turn in the closed end, then accelerating through the seats on the visiting team's side of the field before blasting back out of the open end. I drank hot chocolate and shivered throughout the gray afternoon, sitting in our lower-deck, end-zone seats where the wind never stopped moving.

Everyone who had a ticket that day knew Johnny Unitas had reached his final home game as a Colt. The Colts' new general manager, Joe Thomas, had forced my dad to bench Unitas on the day my dad became the head coach. Thomas wanted to start a new era, one that didn't include Unitas. The era of the "Golden Arm" would end with Unitas standing on the sidelines, a dark blue parka draped over his shoulder pads like bunting on a coffin.

Unitas had taught me to believe in heroes. He was my hero. He made Sundays special. To me, he *was* Sunday.

Once, after Unitas beat the Los Angeles Rams with a winning touchdown drive in the final minute of the game, I watched him walk, his bowlegged strides taking him toward the dugout in the corner of the end zone that led to the Colts' locker room. Unitas waved to his adoring fans, an emperor waving to his loyal subjects.

Just as I had adopted his buzz-cut hairstyle years before, I started to imitate Unitas's bow-legged walk, thinking it might help me become a great quarterback one day. When Jeff Bialzak, one of my friends in the sixth grade at Immaculate Heart of Mary elementary school, told me I looked stupid playing kick ball at recess bowed legged, I punched him in the chest and told him I would punch him again if he told our teacher. Before my threat could have an effect, Ms. Piasecki walked over to us.

"I accidentally kicked the ball in his face," I lied, knowing the truth meant a trip to the principal's office, a call to my parents, a goddamnit look from my father. A lie meant something to add to my next confession, something every student had to do once a week at Immaculate Heart of Mary elementary school. "Bless me father, for I have sinned. I lied about kicking the ball into my friend's face when I actually punched him. I lied so I wouldn't get my father upset at me because he's already upset a lot lately, what with being the Colts head coach and all."

Fortunately, we had a priest in our parish from Italy, Father Cutajar, who had a thick Italian accent and a limited English vocabulary. No matter what sins I confessed, Father Cutajar always gave me the same penance, the Catholic sacrament that completes the forgiveness of sins, a quid pro quo of spiritual cleansing.

"Yes, my child, say three Hail Mary's, two Our Father's, and one Act of Contrition, and go and sin no more," Father Cutajar would say. But in his heavy accent Cutajar's pronouncement of penance sounded more like, "Jes my shield, chay tree el murrays, do ox fudders, and an act of nutrition."

I wondered whether laughing on my way out of the confessional counted as a sin.

I would have gladly signed up for unlimited acts of nutrition from Father Cutajar to avoid seeing Johnny Unitas standing listlessly, like an outsider, on the sidelines of the Colts' final home game of the '72 season against the Buffalo Bills. It seemed an impossibly short stretch of time since Unitas and the Colts had stood atop the NFL as Super Bowl champions.

Two years after the fiasco of Super Bowl III the Colts got their chance at redemption in Super Bowl V, played in the same stadium, Miami's Orange Bowl. Don Shula had left the Colts the year before to coach the

Miami Dolphins, and Don McCafferty, my father's closest friend, had taken over as the Colts' head coach.

Coach McCafferty didn't resemble Don Shula. A tall, slender man, McCafferty smiled a lot, the kind of smile your grandfather gave you, one that makes you feel accomplished even if you haven't done anything but grow a little taller since the last time he saw you. Coach McCafferty gave me that welcoming, easy smile every Saturday when I saw him at Colts practice at Memorial Stadium.

This time the Colts didn't invite coaches and players to bring their children to the Super Bowl. The Colts' owner, Carroll Rosenbloom, thought families had become a distraction leading up to the Colts' loss in Super Bowl III. The biggest upset in NFL history, and they blame the kids. Nice.

It seemed more unusual not to have my mom home during Super Bowl week than my dad. During football season we didn't see Dad much of the week anyway. He worked past nine or ten o'clock most nights. On Thursdays he resurfaced again at home near dinnertime. By that point in the week the anxiety of the upcoming game had a firm grip on my father. Seeing him then didn't seem like a treat.

For my brothers, sister, and me, having both parents out of town meant a visit from my father's mom, Grandmom Lil.

She stood only five feet tall but had the build of a freshly quarried slab of granite, leathery hands, and a face weathered by a long life and a short temper. We called her "Iron Lil," but never to her face.

She had hair like a Brillo pad—short, wiry, rough—and she could comfortably wrap her mouth around cusswords. "Get your scrawny ass over here, right goddamn now." Iron Lil didn't watch my father's games. She had seen him get knocked out once when he played right tackle for the Cleveland Browns in the 1950s, and after promising to "smash the bastard who hit my son," she vowed never to watch his games again, even after his coaching career had taken him to the sidelines.

Iron Lil believed in tough love and wouldn't hesitate to smack me in the back of my head for leaving remnants of roast beef or carrots on my plate. "I didn't spend all day cooking so you could ignore the damn food. Finish."

My dad weighed more than three hundred pounds. It dawned on me he grew to that size on the back of that one word: *Finish*.

By the time Super Bowl V arrived on Sunday, January 17, 1971, I had gained weight, heard the sting of my grandmother's cusswords, and felt the womp of her backhand. Win or lose, my parents would return home the next day and rescue me from my grandmother. This game had a built-in upside.

Tom Landry coached the Cowboys. He wore a suit, tie, and fedora on the sidelines. Landry had the rigid posture and stern expressions I associated with Protestant ministers I had seen while clicking through UHF channels on our TV on Saturday mornings looking for cartoons. I didn't know anything about Protestants or ministers other than the nuns at my school assuring me they were going to hell for not being Catholic. Grandmom Lil echoed the sentiment.

This time the Colts wore white jerseys, not blue, a conspicuous difference from Super Bowl III. The Colts and Cowboys played a messy game. Fumbles, interceptions, and yellow penalty flags littered the field. I grew frustrated, and when my older brother Jim heard me refer to the Cowboys as "goddamn Protestants," he told me to shut up, a command he backed with the threat of his clenched fist. "Just watch the game, guys," my sister, Ruth Ann, pleaded. She had assumed Mom's role as peacekeeper, no easy task in a house with four boys.

"There's Dad," Ruth Ann shouted, happy to redirect our attention. Dad's face appeared larger than life on our new TV, a twenty-five-inch Zenith Chromacolor, a purchase my parents made to assuage our disappointment of not going to this Super Bowl. We all grew quiet at the sight of the goddamnit look.

The first big play came in the second quarter, when Johnny Unitas threw a touchdown pass to Colts tight end John Mackey.

My brothers and I celebrated by burning off our rush of energy with a quick game we called "goal line." My two oldest brothers, Jack and Jim, kneeled on the carpet between the living room and the dining room. The seam in the plush, beige carpet served as the goal line. We tossed cushions from the sofa on the floor behind Jack and Jim to make for a softer landing. Joe played quarterback. Joe and I were the "Little Guys." Jack and Jim the "Big Guys." If we scored, we won. If not, they won. The game had no other rules. Any way we could get across the goal line counted. Any way my older brothers could stop us counted too.

Joe handed off an imaginary football to me. I leaped. Jack smacked my feet while Jim hit my shins, somersaulting through the air across the imaginary goal line into the side of the dining room table, sure I had broken my leg.

"Guys, would you just watch the game?" my sister pleaded.

I hobbled back in front of the TV in time to see Cowboys linebacker Lee Roy Jordan tackle Unitas and force a fumble. The Cowboys recovered.

Dallas took a 13–6 lead into halftime.

During halftime the Big Guys beat the Little Guys so badly in our rematch of goal line football that Iron Lil walked in the room to investigate.

"What in God's holy name are you idiots doing?" she asked, surveying the growing damage in the dining room that now included a broken chair.

"Nothing Grandmom," Jack said. "Gerry just fell down," he said, cutting me a look. "Didn't you?"

I nodded, hoping a nod would slip me past the consequences of a direct lie. I had heard stories of Grandmom Lil taking soap and a scrubbing brush to my father's mouth as a boy for telling a lie. I bobbed my head gently, aiming for a neutral response, one I could defend as either a yes or a no if I had to, fully aware my older brothers would pummel me for contradicting them and Iron Lil would brush a lie right off my face.

"Well, cut it out," Grandmom snapped. "I'm trying to say the damn rosary for your father. How's he doing?" she asked.

"Keep praying, Grandmom," I said. "They're losing."

"To Protestants from Texas, no less," Iron Lil grumbled.

In the second half Unitas didn't return to the game. The hit from Lee Roy Jordan had broken his ribs. The sight of Unitas on the sidelines sent Ruth Ann bolting from the room in tears, retreating to her bedroom with the sobbing protest, "I can't watch this."

But in the fourth quarter the Colts tied the game 13–13, returning hope to our living room. Hope, but not Ruth Ann. When our cheers lured her back from her bedroom, my brothers and I pelted her with our worry: "Get out. You're bad luck. Get back in your room."

An interception by Colts linebacker Mike Curtis with less than two minutes left in the game suddenly put the Colts in a position to win.

"Should we let Ruth Ann watch now?" Joe asked. "It's almost over."

None of us answered, so Ruth Ann inched her way into the living room, sitting in the chair closest to the hallway leading to her bedroom in case she had to make an urgent retreat to salvage the Colts' hopes for a win.

The game came down to field goal attempt. Nine seconds left. Score tied 13–13. The Colts lined up to try a thirty-one-yard field goal with rookie kicker Jim O'Brien.

Jack, Jim, Joe, and I glared at Ruth Ann, letting her know if O'Brien missed, we would blame her. After all, good things happened when she *wasn't* in the room. On television it looked like the rookie kicker faced the most pressure, but my brothers and I knew our sister faced more. Ruth Ann crossed her right leg over her left and gnawed on the fingernails of her left hand while her right hand tapped out the tempo of a muscle spasm against the side of her chair.

Dad often referred to O'Brien as "Lassie," the name of the dog on the eponymous TV show, because O'Brien had long, straight, brown hair that snuck out of the back of his helmet. Long hair had become a dividing line for my father, a demarcation between old ways and new. He hated long hair. It was a protest against authority, the same protest my oldest brother, Jack, had embraced with his long hair, van, tie-died T-shirts, cigarettes;

with dropping out of college; and with the downtown apartment he shared with his girlfriend. Long hair could pull my father out of his recliner to slam his palm into the off button on the TV. He didn't want to see men with long hair protesting a war, men around the age he was when he fought in World War II. My mother insisted if Jack got a bad draft number, he should go to Canada instead of Vietnam. Long hair meant Bob Dylan records played upstairs in our house and Frank Sinatra played downstairs. Long hair meant taking sides. Dad's way—the old way—or Jack's way, the new way.

Jack's long black hair, parted in the middle and flowing back to his shoulder blades, didn't get the benefit of a nickname from our father. It got the goddamnit look.

Long hair had divided us, but now it could unite us.

"He is so cute," Ruth Ann said as the TV cameras zoomed in on a tight shot of Jim O'Brien, his eyes wide, his lips tight, the pulse of panic coursing just beneath the skin on his face.

"Maybe if he makes the kick, you can marry him," I teased.

"And if he doesn't make it, you can plan on an out-of-town wedding, because he's gone," Jim added.

The Colts center snapped the ball, and time stood still. Jim O'Brien took a step toward the ball. I squeezed my fists. O'Brien's right foot thumped into the ball. I held my breath. The kick sailed above the outstretched hands of Cowboys players who slammed into Colts players at the line of scrimmage. I clenched my teeth. The kick was long enough. I shut my eyes. And the room exploded.

"It's good! It's good! It's good!" my brothers shouted.

My parents' bedroom door flew open, and Grandmom Lil charged out. "Jesus Christ, what did you do now?"

"They're going to win! The Colts are going to win!" we shouted.

"Oh mother of God, amen. Praise Jesus," she said.

"There's Dad," Ruth Ann screamed after the game had ended. The camera caught a shot of our father in the swirl of white Colts uniforms near the middle of the field. His grin seemed to stretch nearly as wide as his chest.

Grandmom looked at the TV for the first time and said, "Serves those Protestants right." Then she looked at me and punctuated her smile with a wink.

"This means Dad gets a Super Bowl ring," Jim said. His comment triggered the next competition. One ring, four boys.

"So who inherits—" I began.

"—the ring—" Joe added, picking up my thought.

"—when Dad dies," Jack said, quickly adding, "years and years from now?"

Jim had a solution: "Why don't we play a little goal line and find out?"

Now, with time running out on Johnny Unitas's last home game, a small plane emerged from the matte gray sky over Memorial Stadium, pulling a banner behind it. The banner read, "Unitas We Stand." The fans in Memorial Stadium took their cue. Fifty-eight thousand people stood and gave Unitas a standing ovation.

With a win clearly in hand, I saw my father's usually intense sideline gaze soften. He stood, right hand on his hip, staring through the fog of his breath at the void on the field caused by Unitas's absence from the field, a void caused by the Colts' chain of command.

My father understood orders. He had served in the army in World War II, landing in France as an eighteen-year-old, fighting Germans. Not because he wanted to, but because he was told to. It was his obligation. He was a Catholic. Orders, obligation, and serving higher powers gave him structure, purpose, a way to measure himself. He had drilled the idea into my brothers and me: respect authority, even if you don't agree with it.

With about seven minutes left on the game clock, Colts quarterback Marty Domres limped to the sideline after getting hit on the hip on the last play of the drive. My father put a hand on Domres's shoulder pads and started a brief exchange.

"I want to get John in the game," my father said. "But he won't go in unless you can't play."

"I'm not going to tell him that," Domres answered.

"You don't have to. I will. When you see me talking to him, just point to your hip. I'll take care of the rest."

Domres nodded.

My father's huge frame filled the field of vision in my binoculars as he walked over to Unitas. He said a few words, and Unitas shook his head. Then Unitas looked to Domres, who pointed to his hip and held up both of his palms.

Unitas peeled off his parka, and the sold-out stadium exploded in cheers.

Years later my father shared the conversation with me. Unitas had greeted the news of Domres's injury with a stoic request: "John, I know your hands are tied and I respect that, but don't make me mop up for anyone," Unitas said.

After my father, with Marty Domres's help, had convinced Unitas of the injury, he asked Unitas a question, one that would make my dad smile for the rest of his life any time he recalled the moment: "Wouldn't you like to say good-bye, John?"

Unitas replied by warming up, throwing the football on the sidelines. He had an elegant throwing motion as unique as his black, high-top shoes. He brought the ball back behind his right shoulder, then three-quarters of the way above his head and released it, the football sailing out of his grip just as his right hand moved past the front of his helmet. Even now, far past his prime, his hands worked a football with the confidence of a piano player working a keyboard—the right amount of pressure, the perfect placement, the effortless touch. No longer an athlete in his prime or an artist at his apex, Unitas was now a legend on display.

At the start of the next series Unitas trotted onto the field, a ghost of greatness, no longer young and already immortal. He squatted in his usual place in the huddle, an oval formation of players with his offensive lineman in front of him, running backs and receivers to his left and right.

Unitas handed the ball off twice and, on third down, dropped back to pass. A wall of Bills defensive lineman converged on him. Unitas released the pass. A Bills lineman deflected it, and the pass wobbled in the direction of rookie receiver Eddie Hinton, a pass unworthy of the Unitas's Golden Arm moniker or the legend of a future Hall of Famer, but a pass that would, nonetheless, cap Unitas's career in fitting style. Hinton and two Bills defenders converged on the wobbly throw. The Bills players collided just before the ball arrived, clearing a path for the ball to reach Hinton, who snatched the ball out of the air and ran for a fifty-five-yard touchdown.

Fifty-eight thousand fans unfurled from their seats together and leaped into the shared moment. The man who was Sunday in Baltimore had said his good-bye. The Colts beat the Bills, 35–7.

My dad had a burgundy flush of satisfaction on his cheeks on the drive home from the stadium. From the back of our station wagon I could only pick up snatches of his conversation with my mom, but one line reached me clearly: "If Joe Thomas doesn't like it, he can kiss my ass." My father's grin slipped into the corner of the rearview mirror, as doubts about authority slipped into my mind. I had never liked Joe Thomas to begin with. He had a long, pointy nose and slicked-back hair. From the day he had arrived as my father's new boss, I had suspicions that Satan had found a way to expand his reach from the New York Jets into the Colts organization, a suspicion I didn't share with my father. After all, Joe Thomas was authority. I was supposed to respect that.

The Colts finished the season with a 5–9 record, third place in their division. They won four games and lost five since my father became the head coach. Two of those losses, including the final game of the season, came against the undefeated Miami Dolphins, a team no one had beaten.

Three days after the season ended with David Muir's indecipherable, endless, one-word monologues still ringing in my ears, I learned the Colts had fired my father and the rest of the coaching staff.

That night I retreated to the bedroom I shared with my brother Joe to find my entire world looking as torn apart as my denim-covered school binder that I had flung against the wall earlier in the day, sending papers flying, a storm of English quizzes, math tests, and science notes. The papers cluttered the hardwood floor beneath my chest-high wooden dresser, above which hung a blue and white Baltimore Colts banner. I ripped the banner from the wall.

"Are you going tear up everything you touch tonight?" Joe asked. He lay slumped against the headboard of his bed, his broad cheeks streaked with trails of tears. That night on the six o'clock news we had watched our favorite sportscaster, Vince Bagli, tell the story of the Colts firing our father. Bagli's short, wavy hair looked unkempt, like he had forgotten to run a comb through it after shaking his head over and over from side to side in disbelief of the Colts' demise. "This team was in the AFC Championship last year," he said, his gravelly voice rising, hinting at what Joe and I thought. Who fires their coaching staff a year after that? The press conference with Colts general manager Joe Thomas hurt the most. Thomas never mentioned my father by name. He just strung together clichés: "If you're going to clean house you do it from top to bottom." "We're in a rebuilding phase." I thought I could see a smile lurking beneath his long nose that sloped like President Richard Nixon's. Vince Bagli mentioned something about the president that night, something about Nixon questioning the NFL television plans for the playoffs. The newscast mentioned a story about Vietnam that night too. A plane crash in Chicago. A new play by Neil Simon. They all blurred and blended into background noise for Joe and me, slippery details we couldn't catch or hold on to, details that didn't help explain the only thing we wanted to understand: how, why the Colts would do this to our dad, our family?

Maybe my brother Jack and his friends, who had long hair, wore bell-bottom jeans, and used words like *psychedelic* had a point about not trusting authority.

My father's name, the name I overheard used in nearly every adult conversation I had walked past for the previous three months, was now ignored, discarded, forgotten.

Joe wandered over to the alcove where a dormer window jutted out of the back of our bedroom. He leaned his head against the glass and stared out onto our backyard. We had left our football in the yard, a ball Dad had given us, an official NFL football, the Duke, the only one of its kind in the neighborhood. It lay on the edge of our dormant lawn, a dusting of snow covering it. We had played catch the day before and a game of slow-motion football, one that included the Colts winning another Super Bowl with our dad as head coach. Joe imitated the voice of NFL Films narrator John Facenda's baritone, staccato delivery, overenunciating every consonant for dramatic effect: "In only his second year at the helm, John Sandusky led the storied Colts franchise back to the pinnacle of the pro football world."

Now, an invisible weight of worry replaced our hopes. I felt it in my chest, a heaviness that made it hard to breathe, a tug at the base of my throat, an ache in my knees that poured down to my ankles. I could tell Joe felt it too. He walked over and surrendered to his bed, dropping onto it, arms left dangling over the side, head thrown back onto the pillow, eyes fixed at the ceiling.

"Do you think the Colts might realize they made a mistake and change their mind tomorrow? Maybe hire Dad back?" I asked.

"No," he said with a thud of certainty.

"So what comes next?"

"We go back to school tomorrow, and all the teachers will whisper to each other when we walk by them, like we have some disease they don't want to catch. They'll think they're being nice by telling everyone not to bring up the Colts situation—and they'll give it a sort of code name like that. The Colts situation. Because they won't want to hurt our feelings. Like we have any feelings left after today."

"I always thought Dad would work for the Colts my whole life," I said. He had worked for the Colts since before I was born. I had never rooted for another team, never had another favorite color but blue. I never wanted one. Until now.

On a plastic folding table between our beds we had an electric football game, a rectangular metal game board with twenty-two players, plastic figures half the size of chess pieces, each molded in a full uniform with helmet, jersey, shoulder pads, pants, even tiny black cleats. Each player struck a different football position, left hand forward in a stiff arm, fists meeting in a blocking pose, arms extended for a tackle. Each player stood on a piece of green plastic about the size of a fingertip. When you turned on the switch on the electric cord that ran from the side of the board into a wall socket, the pieces vibrated and moved on the board. When the green base of a player on defense touched the green base of the ball carrier, the player who held a tiny football-shaped piece of felt, the play ended, and you lined up all twenty-two players again, eleven on offense, eleven on defense, in a new formation for the next play.

Our game had the Baltimore Colts in white jerseys and pants and the Green Bay Packers in green jerseys and yellow pants. Joe and I played electric football every day, flipping a coin before each game to see who got stuck with the Packers. Tonight he did.

We lined up players for a kick return as we continued our conversation.

As our game started, the metal field vibrated as loud as an electric razor. A Packer, number twenty-six, shimmied along the thin metal board, moving directly up the middle of the field. "Herb Adderley on the opening kick return," Joe said. We both knew Adderley no longer played for the Packers. Green Bay had traded him three years before, but in the timeless world of electric football, we controlled who played and who coached. Joe reached across the board and flicked a Colts player out of the way. "He gets a great block," Joe explained. Normally I would have protested or thrown a Packers player at Joe, but instead I laughed for the first time that day at the sight of a Colts player flying off the field and caroming with a plink off our desk light before falling to the hardwood floor.

Then I began helping Joe. I picked up a Colts player and threw it across the room. "Another great block." Joe took the palm of his right hand and leveled a line of Colts players, leaving them vibrating in circles as Herb Adderley continued moving across the field.

I leaned in, ready to smack another Colts player from the board when the sight of the tiny blue number on the player's jersey squeezed a short burst of air from my chest. The player in Herb Adderley's metal path was a defender with outstretched arms, wearing number seventy-eight. Bubba Smith. Joe and I loved Bubba.

After Saturday practices at Memorial Stadium we would bring grape and orange sodas to Bubba's locker from the vending machine in the locker room and would talk to Bubba while he sat on a short, three-legged wooden stool, combing his afro with a long, metal pick. Bubba stood six feet, seven inches tall, the biggest man either Joe or I had ever seen. He had smooth, dark skin, the color of roasted chestnuts, and a black mustache that wrapped around his thick lips in a permanent scowl. When my father would come looking for us to tell us it was time to go home, Bubba would nod in his direction and whisper to us, "Better get going. None of us want to make that man mad."

I couldn't push Bubba out of Herb Adderley's way. We turned off the game instead.

"Think we'll ever see Bubba again?" I asked.

"Who knows," Joe said. He paused before adding something neither of us had ever considered before: "Dad doesn't even know what's going to happen next."

I walked over to the window and stared out at our backyard. An uneven streak of moonlight spilled through the cloudy night sky, casting a silver haze across the football we had left in the yard. The ball looked as lost as Joe and I felt.

— Chapter Five —

THE SIDELINES

The next season my father took a job as the offensive line coach of the Philadelphia Eagles, a homecoming of sorts, as he grew up in South Philly. According to the odometer on my dad's Chrysler Cordoba, our new house in South Jersey stood 112 miles from Baltimore, but the emotional distance was much further. The move cleaved our family in half. Jack, my oldest brother, had recently married. Jim and Ruth Ann, next in the age pecking order, stayed behind in Baltimore to go to college.

Only Joe and I moved with my parents to South Jersey. That summer, just before I began eighth grade, Joe would share with me the magic of seeing our father up close at work for the first time, all the while trying to remain invisible ourselves, working in the Philadelphia Eagles' training camp.

Mike McCormick, the head coach of the Eagles, had remained close friends with my dad since they played together with the Cleveland Browns in the 1950s.

McCormick had graying hair, a bulbous nose, and a reddish, round face that looked well acquainted with a bottle of beer, and like my dad, he had hands the size of holiday hams. Together they resembled a pair of Irish cops walking their beat.

A devout Catholic and family man, Coach McCormick let each assistant coach bring his teenage sons to training camp to work as ball boys. A ball boy was a gopher, as in "go for this," "go for that." Ten of us arrived to work under the equipment manager, Rusty Sweeney, doing the least glamorous jobs surrounding a football team: picking up dirty uniforms in the locker room, washing and folding towels, cleaning up the practice field, and answering yes to anything else Rusty demanded in between the coffee-colored streams of tobacco juice he spat on the ground.

Earlier in the summer my father had told Joe he could work training camp, but he said nothing to me until one evening when I was lying in Joe's room, reading my brother's copy of *The Exorcist*, wondering, *Is this stuff real or just a scare tactic?* Joe suspected a bit of both; my father never doubted the church.

"What in the hell are you doing reading that book?" my father asked after walking into Joe's room unannounced. *Did houses in New Jersey not have doors? Where did he come from? How does a three-hundred-pound man just appear?* I thought. "You're not old enough to read that. Put it away," my father said.

I snapped the paperback shut, cringing at not marking the page, wondering whether Satan loses in the end and how long it would take me now to find out. My father stopped in the doorway on his way out of the room and flashed me the quickest of grins, one that snuck under the book censure lingering in his eyes. "But you are old enough to go to training camp as a ball boy," he said.

The Eagles trained at Weidner College, a small school in West Chester, Pennsylvania, about twenty-five minutes from Veterans Stadium in Philadelphia. It was the summer I got a real education, not with books and classes but with life experience.

Coach McCormick had a son, Timmy, who was Joe's age, and he took a leadership role among the ball boys, especially when it came to managing the schedule for phone duty. Every evening after dinner, when coaches and players gathered for meetings, two ball boys reported to the coaches' dormitory to answer phone calls and take messages for the coaches.

During the first week of camp Timmy McCormick, a tall, lanky high school sophomore, outlined the importance of the job. He stood in front of the group, his left foot resting on a plastic laundry basket filled with a dirty jeans, T-shirts, and socks. In his left hand he held a stack of pink phone message slips. In his right hand he had a whiteboard with a crude drawing of the layout of the coaches' dorm, a three-story building on the opposite side of the campus from the ball boys' dorm.

Timmy walked us through his map, circling with a red marker an area in the middle. "Here you'll find a refrigerator stocked with beers. And one floor down," he pointed to the bottom of the map, "a washer and dryer." Timmy grinned, the corners of his mouth sliding farther and farther apart. "Coaches know about beer. They know nothing about laundry. That's our in."

Timmy had overheard his father arranging a deal with a local beer distributor, a passionate Eagles fan, to stock the coaches' refrigerator with Budweiser. When the refrigerator ran low on beer, the distributor would automatically restock it. Simple.

One ball boy would pay attention to the phone. The other would do laundry, which, when washed, dried, folded, and placed in the basket Timmy provided, perfectly concealed a case of beer. When coaches returned to their dorm, the ball boys would leave with clean clothes and cold beer. Timmy posted a phone duty schedule for ball boy tandems, and we went about the business of answering phones, folding laundry, and stealing beer. His plan was so good that it created a problem even Timmy couldn't predict.

Rusty Sweeney expected us in the locker room by 7:30 a.m. A short, gritty Texan who took his nickname from his hair color, Rusty had his first wad of chewing tobacco tucked in his cheek by the time we arrived each morning. After plunking a stream of tobacco juice into the brass spittoon on the floor next to his desk, Rusty would greet us with his daily mantra: "Set up, clean up, shut up. That's what I expect from you today."

The locker room at Widener College sat in a valley half a mile from the practice field. Ball boys made the trip twice a day to the practice field in the back of Rusty's three-wheeled, flat-bed utility cart. Coach

McCormick gave Rusty specific orders: no players in the cart. He didn't want a player falling off the cart and getting hurt. Safety rules didn't apply to coaches' sons, however. We didn't translate into wins or losses.

Rusty preferred Timmy's interpretation of the rule: don't let Coach McCormick *see* any players in the cart. On the trip from the locker room to the field, if Rusty came across a player he liked, he would tell me, the youngest ball boy, to get off the cart to make room for the player. Rusty would let the player off a block from the field so it looked like he had walked all the way, and then he'd shout back to me to "Catch the fuck up!"

The first time Rusty said that to me he mistook my blank expression for surprise.

"Come here," he said, curling his index finger toward him as I reached the back of the cart. "This is football camp. Man up." Then he spit a stream of tobacco juice between my white sneakers to punctuate his point.

It didn't take me long to learn that, like everything else in football, use of the f-word had clear rules—in this case unwritten, but so clear that they could have just as easily appeared in the official NFL rulebook:

Usage of the F-word

1. The f-word shall only be used by an individual/employee of an NFL team when that individual/employee addresses someone of equal or lesser rank in the organizational flow chart.

   a. A ball boy can direct the f-word to another ball boy, but a ball boy cannot use the word f-word in response to an equipment manager, player, or coach's demands.

   b. The head coach can use the f-word while instructing, arguing, or encouraging his assistant coaches or players. For example:

   "We're going to run that fucking play until we get it right."

    c. An assistant coach should not use any form of the f-word
        while addressing the head coach. An assistant coach
        can,however, use the f-word while comparing notes with
        another assistant coach or evaluating a player. For example:
        "That guy can't fucking play for us."

2. As long as it is used in the proper chain of command, coaches,
players, ball boys, or other organization members/employees can
use the f-word for any of the following purposes:

    a. A compliment: "Nice fucking play."

    b. A prediction: "We'll kick their fucking ass."

    c. An indirect complaint shared with a peer but not
        delivered to a supervisor: "Fuck him if he thinks I'm
        switching positions."

    d. A shared sense of misery: "It's fucking hot out here today."

3. No member of an NFL organization shall use the f-word or
its commonly associated hand gestures while talking to or
about fans.

The Eagles' training camp practices lasted about two hours. Before each practice Rusty assigned a ball boy to each position coach with instructions to make sure the coach and his players had all the equipment, towels, and water they needed and, for anything more complicated, to find Rusty.

On the second week of training camp Rusty assigned me to work the morning practice with my dad and his offensive linemen. Without knowing it, Rusty had peeled back a corner of fatherhood, affording me a glimpse of the man behind it. No less than half an hour earlier in the locker room my father greeted me like he hadn't seen me for weeks. He had a broad grin, nearly as bright as his white Eagles baseball cap. He smacked me on the back, a concussive thud. His look lingered—not the inspection stare I had seen many times in the past nor the look of disappointment at my skinny arms and legs jutting out from oversized sleeves and shorts; instead, this was a happy look, a flush of red in his round face, a glint in his eyes. My father's aura of happiness expanded along with the sweat stains that expanded in half-moons beneath the arms of his gray T-shirt as he pushed his players through practice drills.

His linemen practiced driving out of their stances at the snap of the ball and pushing a blocking sled that my father stood on, barking instructions and encouragement.

"Drive it, drive it, drive it! C'mon, move the damn thing! Go, go, go! Good job."

My father's instructions melded into a stream of commands and demands of the other coaches nearby:

"Backside. Backside."

"Here we go. On two, on two."

"Adjust out of red formation."

"Set. Eighty. Eighty. Hut."

"Scrape the tackle. Don't hang up there."

My father packed a broad spectrum of information into each breath—instruction, encouragement, adjustment, reinforcement. "Hit it hard. Drive. You can do it. Harder. Move your feet. Harder. Drop your hips. *Inhale.* Set a little left. Move. Don't stop. Lower. Feet. Good job. *Inhale.*" A poor effort or a missed block by one of my father's linemen triggered corrections, more teaching, but not the irritation I saw cloud his face when he cleaned the basement at home or paid the bills while sitting at the kitchen table, squeezing the pen and clenching his jaw as a low growl as from shifting tectonic plates rose from the depths of his massive body.

"Gerry, hop on the sled," my father said, exchanging his three hundred pounds for my scrawny frame. Then he lined up next to the Eagles left tackle, Jerry Sizemore, to demonstrate a blocking technique. When my father lunged into the blocking sled, slamming his shoulder into the padding, the sled rose up, knocking me off balance. I clutched the iron bar in front of me, fighting against the feeling that I was about to catapult off the back of the sled. Sizemore tried to mimic the move. I gripped the bar tighter, preparing for another blast, but Sizemore lost his footing and barely made contact with the three-foot-tall pad on the blocking sled. He slammed his fist into the grass and shouted, "Mother fucker," followed by a sheepish glance and apology to my father: "Sorry, John." I couldn't tell whether he apologized for the poor block or the language, but my father knew. He cut Sizemore off with a smile. I was in their world—no apologies needed; get used to it. (See "Usage of the F-word," section 2d.) As Sizemore reset in a blocking stance, the front of his right foot even with the instep of his left foot, the fingertips of his right hand set in grass, my father crouched next to him, directly in front of me, with his smile now gone. "Ready. Set," my father barked, the first word, *ready*, stretching out long and slow like he was buying time to gather his thoughts. The second word, *set*, a short, crisp command. His eyes darted from Sizemore to me. Then my father said with the same emphasis he had placed on *set*—the force of a ball peen hammer striking a nail head: "Just remember, we *never* use that language around Mom." Before I could respond, my father shouted "hut," and Sizemore exploded into the blocking sled, lifting the metal contraption into the air while I gripped the back of the sled to avoid flying five yards down field.

That night, with the ball boys gathered around him, willing acolytes at his altar of adventure, Timmy McCormick announced, "Tonight we chew tobacco."

Timmy had pilfered a few bags of chewing tobacco from Rusty's desk. Timmy reached into the foil bag and pulled out a wad of chewing tobacco. I had never seen it up close. It looked like moist, dark brown spinach. He stuffed the tobacco in his right cheek.

"Just let it sit there. You don't really chew it," Timmy instructed. "And when you feel like you have to spit," Timmy then demonstrated, launching a brown stream from his mouth into a green paper cup with Gatorade written on the side, another pickup from the equipment room.

Timmy passed around the foil pouch of Red Man chewing tobacco first to John Idzik Jr., the son of the running backs coach—and future New York Jets general manager—then to Tad Wampfler, the defensive line coach's son, and then to my brother Joe.

By the time the pouch reached me, the rest of the ball boys had begun spitting into their own paper cups. On my first attempt to spit I launched the entire wad of tobacco off the rim of my cup, splattering the tobacco and what little spit accompanied it onto the floor near John Idzik's feet.

"Idiot!" Idzik yelled.

"Relax," Timmy said. "You screw up, you clean up."

Mopping up the leafy brown goop made me swear off the evils of tobacco, an oath that lasted for one day.

The next night we chewed tobacco again. This time I got the spitting part right, and I discovered the allure of the habit: it makes your head spin. "Whew," I announced. "This here stuff is good. Damn good."

"Some reason you're speaking with a Texas accent?" Joe asked.

The rest of the ball boys cracked up laughing, so I played to the audience. "Damn straight. A good chaw can flat out change a man."

"Yeah, it can make him turn green. Spit it out, Gerry. Hurry," Timmy said.

My head had begun spinning faster and faster. The mouth of my paper cup moved in circles in front of me as I tried to drop the wad of tobacco, careful not to plop it in like a billiard ball this time.

A wave of nausea pushed up from my stomach to my throat.

"Lay down, Tex," Timmy said.

I had a second chance to quit and, despite my second vow to never touch the stuff, I would end up regretting not living up to my word.

Within a few nights our chewing tobacco parties had become ritual, but they had also created a problem. Timmy lifted the sheets that draped over the side of his bed and revealed cases of Budweiser. "We have too much beer," he said. "I have two more cases in my closet. If my father or Rusty ever comes to this room, how will I explain all this beer?" Chewing tobacco had replaced drinking beer. So he came up with a plan, one I would quickly regret hearing, where we could do both.

"The offensive lineman from Texas showed me this," Timmy said, as he put a wad of tobacco in his mouth, spit, then took a long drink from his can of beer. "The trick is to spit, then drink your beer before your mouth fills up with tobacco juice again."

Joe followed Timmy's lead, which was the only encouragement I needed. I followed Joe. The last thing I remembered was my head spinning, spinning, faster, faster, at an accelerating pace, the room wrapping around me. I saw the bed, Joe, Timmy, beer, bed, Joe, Timmy beer, bed, Joe, blank.

I came to with my head bobbing above a toilet, vomiting beer and tobacco. I had swallowed the entire tobacco wad.

When I showed up in the locker room the next morning Rusty laughed each time I retreated to the bathroom to retch more. He told my father he needed my help in the equipment room that morning in order to explain why I wasn't on the practice field.

Rusty left me to the task of folding towels with Andrew Frankel, the one ball boy who wasn't a coach's son and didn't fit into our loose fraternity. Coaches' sons understand each other. We understand Sunday isn't a day of rest. It's a day of work, a day that dictates the rest of the week and most of your life. We understand our fathers spend more time with other people's sons than their own. But Andrew Frankel did not understand, and I did not understand him. He came from another world, a world with a father who wasn't a coach. According to Andrew, his father "was a friend of the team owner. He worked with lots of money, had something to do with banking."

How could a fourteen-year-old not know what his father did for a living? Every coach's son knows exactly what his father does. A coach's son memorizes his father's bio in the team's media guide. He knows how many Pro Bowl players his father has coached, how long his father has coached, how many championship rings he has at home in the top drawer of his dresser.

Andrew only knew his father had something to do with money, nothing more than that—no details, no shared memories, no identity behind the word *dad*. That seemed to me like not having a father at all.

Andrew was skinnier than me. He had a narrow face, wavy brown hair, and a large, hooked nose that looked borrowed from the face of a sixty-year-old man.

That day, as my urge to vomit subsided, Andrew and I worked through a mountain of towels, folding and stacking them, a routine that kept us three feet apart from each other, standing on opposite sides of a wooden table next to the stainless-steel industrial clothes dryer. As we folded and stacked the towels it become more awkward to stay silent than it was to find something to talk about.

"You don't seem like you're having much fun this summer," I said.

He reached into the massive metal dryer and pulled out more towels.

"Not quite what I'm used to," he said.

"And what's that?"

"My parents usually send me to a Jewish youth camp. They thought I would enjoy this more," he said, rolling his eyes at their stupidity.

"You'd rather spend your summer with Jewish kids than in an NFL training camp?" I asked incredulously.

Andrew looked over a stack of towels and said, "You've never . . ."

Then he stopped, shaking his head.

"Never what?"

"Never been around a Jew before, have you?"

I stared at him, trying to think of some way to avoid telling Andrew he was right.

Andrew continued talking, his voice carrying the weight of sadness, the distant sound of thoughts insulated with homesickness. "It's not contagious, you know, being Jewish. Even if everyone around here, at least all the other ball boys, act like it."

With all of the towels folded and Rusty out on the practice field, Andrew and I had nothing to do but sit across from each and continue our conversation.

"What other stuff did you do in Jew . . . in, uh, your camp?" I asked.

"Usual camp stuff. Hiking, camping, lying about girls."

"We do a lot of that in Timmy McCormick's room. The lying part. Not so much with the hiking and camping," I said, laughing at my own joke, until Andrew's comment silenced me.

"I wouldn't know."

We had ostracized Andrew by never inviting him to join us in anything, all without a single word said.

"Do anything else fun in your old camp?" I asked.

"Sometimes, late at night, some of us would sneak off and drink beer. Skinny as I am, I can drink a lot of beer."

Then I had an idea.

That night, after I returned to my dorm, I stopped by Andrew's room and told him to follow me. When the two of us walked into Timmy's room, silence and stares greeted us.

Joe slipped the beer in his right hand under the pillow on Timmy's bed. He turned a wide-eyed stare toward me, an accusing look.

"Relax," I said. "Andrew is going to help us solve your problem, Timmy."

Timmy ran his hand across the front of his hair, never taking his eyes off Andrew, who had yet to say a word.

I reached into the small refrigerator next to Timmy's bed, pulled out a beer, and handed it to Andrew with a nod. He pulled off the tab and chugged the beer in one steady gulp, followed by a massive belch. Then he reached for another. By the time Andrew had sucked down four beers, Joe had moved off the bed and placed a hand on Andrew's shoulder, then his stomach, checking to see how Andrew's narrow frame could accommodate so much beer.

"What did you say your name was?" Timmy asked.

"Andrew. Andrew Frankel."

"Welcome, Andrew Frankel. We get together every night around ten. How are you with chewing tobacco?"

By the end of the night Andrew had not only become part of the group; he had also agreed to the newest part of Timmy's plan: he was in charge of sneaking beer back into the coaches' refrigerator.

The next day, when I saw my father on the practice field, I wanted to tell him about the experience the night before. I wanted him to look at me with the smile in his eyes that he poured onto a rookie lineman who perfectly executed the footwork of a trap block—reach, pivot, step, bend, explode, followed by the snap of my father's clap: "That's it. That's it. Way to go." I settled for a slap on my back when my father welcomed me back to the practice field. I suspected he had no idea how much I had changed since the first day of training camp.

The end of camp segued into the start of football season. On Sundays in the fall the ball boys reunited for home games at Philadelphia's Veterans Stadium. We wore blue jeans, Eagles sweatshirts, baseball caps, and black vests with a neon orange X on the front and back. The vests made it easier for officials to spot us on the field.

Three ball boys worked each sideline: one at the line of scrimmage, one ten yards in front of the line of scrimmage, and one about thirty yards down field. If a play ended outside of the hash marks, the short, parallel white lines running down the middle of the field like stitches, an official would signal to the nearest ball boy to throw him a football, which he placed on the hash mark for the start of the next play.

My first turn to work the sidelines came on a cold Sunday afternoon in early October of the '73 season. The Eagles faced the Dallas Cowboys. Standing on the field during the singing of the national anthem, I felt a plunging sensation that began just below my chest and dropped through my stomach, thighs, knees, calves, and out through the bottom of my feet, an almost electric current of fear, a freefall of anxiety.

I worked the Cowboys side of the field, ten yards away from my brother Joe. On the first play of the game Eagles running back Tom Sullivan ran the ball in my direction, sweeping around the right side of the Eagles offensive line, colliding head first with Dallas lineman Bob Lilly with a loud crack that dropped Sullivan to the ground, skidding on the turf, stopping inches from my feet. The numbness of shock began to wrap around me after nearly getting run over on the first play of the game. An official began screaming at me, which snapped me out of it. He wanted a football.

Before the game Rusty had stressed to me, using rules one through three of the NFL rulebook's "Usage of the F-word," to always lob the ball to officials underhanded. Always underhand—always. Easier for them to catch. They get booed if they don't catch the ball.

But the referee who wanted the ball now stood in the middle of the field, in between the hash marks. I couldn't lob a ball underhanded thirty yards. My heart pounded. Was I allowed to run out closer to him? Rusty didn't tell me that.

"Throw the damn ball!" the official shouted.

I stood frozen, turning toward Joe, looking for advice, but a group of Cowboys players had gathered around Bob Lilly to celebrate his tackle and blocked my view of Joe. The ref screamed again, veins bulging in his neck, blue striations beside his Adam's apple.

I let the ball fly. Overhand.

I watched my throw arc in a perfect spiral as it sailed fifteen feet over the official's head, bounced, and rolled to the other side of the field, directly in front of my father. I hoped his look of disappointment—eyes rolling, cheeks puffed, a long exhale—was because of Sullivan's run and not my throw.

At halftime I followed the Eagles off the field. A salty, copper smell of sweat and blood filled the locker room. I darted around, filling players' demands for everything from Gatorade to towels to equipment. A chinstrap for Roman Gabriel. Helmet cheek pad for linebacker John Bunting. New sock for Tom Sullivan.

Coaches huddled with players, diagramming strategy adjustments in complicated language. "If the defense shifts into an over front, expect to see a weak side roll to cover two if we're not in the red zone."

On the walk back to the field for the second half the click-clack of cleats filled the narrow, concrete tunnel leading from the locker room to the field, the cadence of a marching army. Rusty walked up beside me and told me to switch to the Eagles side in the second half. "That way, if you fuck up again, I can kill you faster," he said, spitting a stream of tobacco juice a split-second ahead of and in the exact spot of my next step.

I saw my dad as I reached the Eagles bench. "Having fun?" he asked, slipping on his headset. I nodded, relieved he didn't bring up my throw. He turned his attention to his linemen sitting on the bench. "Remember the hard count. Don't flinch . . ." My dad's voice had a certainty to it. It resonated confidence, a confidence I could never imagine having myself.

The second half started more smoothly. By the fourth quarter my panic had subsided, and I had stretched the range of my underhand toss to the hash mark.

Late in the game Roman Gabriel threw a pass to Eagles tight end Charles Young near the sideline. It was so close to me that I could see the sweat on Young's face and his jaundiced eyes grow wide as the ball landed in his hands. I could feel the collision as Cowboys safety Charlie Waters slammed into Young's back, the way you feel a quick crack of thunder in an electrical storm. I could see Young flying out of bounds, his feet lifted from the ground. I could see the tear in Young's jersey by his shoulder pads and scuff mark on the side of his helmet. And a sliver of a second too late, I realized I could see it all too closely.

The next thing I remember, I was sitting on the Eagles bench as the team doctor waved an ammonia capsule under my nose. Eagles players filed past the bench toward the locker room. My dad's face slowly came into focus. His voice had the soft, stretchiness of taffy. He said something that sounded like concussion, three long syllables in slow motion. He seemed unusually happy. Had I done something to make him proud? He helped me off the bench, his thick, right arm wrapped around my back, guiding, practically carrying me to the locker room, where he handed me off to Joe, who filled me in on the secret to my father's joy.

The Eagles had upset the Cowboys 30–16.

By my father's third year with the Eagles, losses outnumbered wins and upset celebrations had become a distant memory. When the Eagles started the season with a 1–5 record, conversations in our house took on a short-term focus, nothing about next summer or next fall.

I could feel my father growing more tense by the day, and I scrambled to find topics other than football to talk about with him. After going with him to a Saturday practice, as he pulled out of his parking space beneath the stadium, I asked him whether he ever worried about hitting the large concrete support beam next to his parking space. He glared at me and grumbled, "Why would I hit something I've parked next to for three years?"

Joe cleared his throat loudly in the backseat, signaling me to slink away from the topic. "Are the Rams as good as their record?" Joe asked Dad, trying to redirect the conversation away from the landmine I had brushed up against.

"Probably better," he said, a sense of doom lingering in his words.

The Los Angeles Rams were 5–1. The Eagles would play them in two days on Monday Night Football, a chance to turn Philadelphia's season around in the national spotlight or to seal the fate of a season already falling apart.

"Maybe a chance for an upset," I chirped, regretting immediately stepping into a football topic. I felt Joe kick the back of my seat. My father didn't even turn his head in my direction as he drove down Broad Street. He didn't seem to understand my faith in his abilities as a football coach. But I understood the silence that consumed our car ride as my father drove across the Walt Whitman Bridge toward our home in South Jersey.

The Rams destroyed the Eagles.

Late in the game, when Eagles quarterback Mike Boryla threw an interception, Rams linebacker Isiah Robertson sprinted by Joe and me on the sidelines as we watched him run seventy-six yards for a touchdown that made the final score 42–6.

"What do you think this means?" I asked my big brother.

"It means we're moving."

At the end of the game I cleaned up the Rams' bench area, gathered the three bags filled with game balls that Rusty had put me in charge of, and walked across the field toward the Eagles' locker room. I wouldn't get there without more trouble.

Six guys surrounded me at midfield. They all looked like they were in their twenties.

"Give us the balls, kid," one of the guys said. He wore a dark leather jacket and had a Fu Manchu mustache that covered crooked, yellow teeth. His breath reeked of beer. The group closed in, all six standing within an arm's length of me. I looked around for a cop, a player, a coach, Joe—anyone who could help me—but all I could see were six drunk faces, all getting closer, all talking now, all telling me to give up the balls. I clutched the three bags of footballs tighter, lowered my head, and tried to push my way through the ring of men. A punch struck me in the side of my head just beneath my left eye and knocked me to one knee. A second punch found my stomach. Another punch to the back of my head. I stumbled forward and lost my balance. The six men descended on me, trying to wrestle the bags free from my arms. Another blow to my face, the side of my head, my back, ribs. I couldn't raise a fist to protect myself without losing my grip on the bags. Through a tangle of legs I could see my brother, Timmy McCormick, John Idzik Jr., and Andrew Frankel running full speed toward me.

They slammed into the pack, knocking the men off me. Joe grabbed the guy in the leather jacket and buckled his knees with a punch to his face that spurted blood from the man's nose and mouth. When the drunk scrambled to his feet and tried to run, Joe grabbed his leather jacket, ripping it halfway up the back and slowing his exit just enough for a group of cops to arrive and shove the man down onto the cold Veterans Stadium turf.

I sprinted, with the football bags still in my grasp, to the locker room within the safety of a gauntlet of ball boys. We barreled through the locker room doors so loudly Coach McCormick interrupted his postgame talk to the players to ask what the hell was going on. Timmy quickly explained what happened. Then Coach McCormick turned his attention back to the Eagles players and said, "I stand corrected. One member of this team did not turn the goddamn ball over tonight. Well done, Gerry."

I looked to the left of Coach McCormick and saw my father smiling for the first time that night. Unfortunately his smile didn't last very long. An hour later, as we left the stadium, my father, pulling out of his parking space, slammed the front left fender of his car into the concrete support beam next to his parking spot. He whipped his head around and stared at me in the backseat, volcanic steam simmering in his eyes. His lips curled back from his clenched teeth. Before he could say a word, my mother intervened. "John, it was an accident," she said. "And he didn't cause it."

As we drove in silence again across the Walt Whitman Bridge, I wondered where we would live the following football season.

Chapter Six

LEGENDS

The next season my father took a job as the offensive line coach with his old boss from Baltimore, Don Shula, now the head coach of the Miami Dolphins, and we moved to South Florida.

Two years earlier the Dolphins had won their second Super Bowl. I thought my father had joined a team on par with royalty. Then we got to South Florida.

I couldn't understand why my father seemed so happy as he drove Joe and me to the Dolphins facility for the first time. The Dolphins trained at Biscayne College, a small Catholic college in Opa-locka, a neighborhood just north of Miami. Squatty, one-story houses with barrel-tile roofs, stucco walls, and windows covered by crime bars lined flat, straight streets dotted with scrubby palm trees and neglected lawns of rocks and sand with an occasional thatch of grass. The training facility looked as bleak and run-down as the neighborhood. A one-story, white stucco building next to a parking lot pocked with crumbling asphalt on the backside of the college's property, from the outside the facility looked more like a chop shop than an NFL team headquarters.

"Waddya you think?" my father asked.

I looked at Joe, trusting him to think of an appropriate lie to mask our disappointment.

Training camp in Miami had as different of an atmosphere from Philadelphia as the landscape. Don Shula treated everyone the same whether you coached for him, played quarterback, or picked up towels and tape in the locker room. Shula's expectations rivaled the intensity of South Florida sunshine.

I learned that the hard way.

During the first day of training camp Shula tested how far his players could run in twelve minutes, how fast they could run a forty-yard dash, how high they could jump from a standing start, how quickly they could run between orange cones set five and ten yards apart, and how quickly they could recover. He measured everything and timed every movement and instructed me to keep track of it all on a clipboard.

I sprinted from station to station, sweating almost as much as the players, collecting all the information Coach Shula told me he wanted. At the end of the day I approached Coach Shula as he walked off the field with my dad and asked what he wanted me to do with the test results.

"Don't care," Shula said, not breaking his jaunty, slightly pigeon-toed stride.

I stood confused for a quick moment on the neatly manicured practice field before jogging to catch up with my father and Coach Shula. My father grinned and explained, "We only test the players so they'll stay in shape in the off-season."

"We don't care about their scores." Then Shula added, "This afternoon we put on pads and find out who can play football."

My father gave me a conspirator's wink. For the first time in my life he let me in on a secret his players didn't know.

I shared a room with my dad in the two-story dormitory across the parking lot from the Dolphins' training facility. It resembled a truck stop motel. Beige paint peeled off cinderblock walls inside and outside of the rooms. Rust covered more of the railings and exposed metal on the stairwells and balconies than the eggshell colored paint that flaked off in pieces the size of silver dollars.

Joe didn't sleep at training camp. He drove home each evening to keep our mom company and to shuttle her back and forth to camp. In Miami my mom put her sewing skills to work to give my father's players a competitive advantage: tighter jerseys that defensive players couldn't grab and hold. In between morning and afternoon practices she set up a makeshift seamstress shop in the room my dad and I shared. She looked like a tailor from the garment district in New York as she measured players: straight pins clenched in her front teeth, a measuring tape draped around her neck, a stick of chalk in her hand, and reading glasses resting on the slope of her button of a nose, waiting for players to arrive.

Bob Keuchenberg, Larry Little, Jim Langer, and the rest of my father's offensive linemen arrived one by one to get fitted. Mom also set up for the players a small buffet of split pea soup, turkey and ham sandwiches, chocolate chip and butterscotch cookies—her way to make them feel more at home. They did, after all, have to listen to Dad and Coach Shula all day. Joe or I would retrieve each player's game jerseys from the equipment room, and Mom would begin tailoring them. A day or two later, when she had finished a jersey, my dad sent the player back to my mom for a final fitting—and another pass through her buffet line—to ensure each jersey fit as tight as an undershirt, with no loose clothing for a defensive player to grab or hold.

It didn't take long for my mom's sewing skills and her pea soup to lure other players to the dorm room between practices. Jim Mandich, a tight end, had a pair of dress pants that needed altering. Don Nottingham, a running back, wanted tighter sleeves on his jersey. Larry Seiple, the punter, just wanted the soup.

My mother had created more than a fitting room and buffet. A bond evolved between our family and the Dolphins players. Dad coached them. Joe and I cleaned up after them. Mom cooked and sewed for them. We all had a role, and we all got to spend time together and listen to Dad snore through his fifteen-minute nap between practices, undisturbed by the whirring sound of Mom's sewing machine engine. She had created a little oasis, a respite from the demands of Don Shula's training camp. Players loved to talk to her while they ate her soup. She would give them her full attention while they talked about the girlfriend, the wife, the parents they missed. She could carry on a conversation without saying a word, her animated eyebrows steepling in surprise, one arching and the other lowering in a look of disbelief, both knitting together above the bridge of her thin nose in tight focus and concentration. She would sew and listen. The players would eat and talk.

Before each practice the Dolphins' equipment manager, Dan Dowd, a man with a puckish grin and mop of white hair, sent a ball boy to Coach Shula for instructions. The Dolphins had two practice fields. If Coach Shula planned on a full-contact scrimmage, he would indicate which field needed first down markers and orange end-zone pylons.

The first time Dan sent me to Coach Shula's office I saw Coach leaning back in his leather chair, talking on the phone. Afraid to interrupt him, I stood in his doorway gawking at the sports museum in front of me. Plaques covered the paneled wall behind Shula's sprawling desk. Coach of the Year. *Time* magazine Man of the Year. Team of the Century. The Perfect Season. Framed photographs of Coach Shula with celebrities sat along the edges of his desk: President Nixon, Elizabeth Taylor, Jack Nicklaus. Trophy cases lined two other walls of his office. The fourth wall, a floor-to-ceiling sliding-glass door, looked across a pool onto the practice fields.

Shula eventually sensed my presence, glanced over his shoulder, and held up his right index finger. Field one. Got it.

I set up field one with Joe and Coach Shula's two sons, David, who was Joe's age, and Michael, who was a couple of years younger than me. The four of us played catch as we waited for practice to begin. I didn't have to wait long to find out why everyone enjoyed a respite from Don Shula.

Shula led players on a jog around the far goal post toward the middle of the practice fields. He wore tight-fitting, aqua coaching shorts and a white collared shirt with the Dolphins logo on the front, a porpoise wearing a white helmet as it jumped in front of an orange outline of the sun. As Coach Shula approached the middle of the field Michael and David started inching away. Danger. We all saw the jaw. When he got closer I could see steam coming from fissures that were his deep-set eyes beneath straight-edge eyebrows; it made my legs weak. He had a perfectly balanced face and short dark hair, framed by long sideburns, his chin an equilateral triangle—the Vitruvian Coach, ready to explode.

He shouted while looking directly at me, "Who's the goddamn idiot who set up field one?"

I could feel the stares of players gathering behind Shula. I saw my dad out of the corner of my eye. He looked down.

Shula repeated his question in a heated, staccato pace. "Who's . . . the goddamn . . . idiot . . . who set up . . . field . . . one?"

I pointed at his son Mike and said, "I think he did it."

A grin diffused the steam from Coach Shula's eyes as he began to laugh. "Good one, Ger," he said. The players' laughter followed a second later.

Don Strock, the backup quarterback, jogged past me and said from the corner of his mouth, "Lucky he didn't kill you for that."

My dad walked up next to me and grinned. "Bet you feel like crapping yourself right about now," he said.

I looked at him and said, "I think I just did."

After our first year in South Florida Joe left for college on a football scholarship to Tulsa. By the time training camp had arrived for my father's third year with the Dolphins, it also called my brother away. As Joe and I drove to the airport we laughed about the trouble we both knew I would get in with Dad because I didn't have Joe around as my buffer when football season put Dad's mood on edge.

"Remember when he used to make us pick up rocks in the yard?" Joe said, his laughter forcing him to cough and bend over, hands on knees, to catch his breath. Each summer Dad and the rest of the coaches had off for the entire month of June. He didn't golf, and he had no hobbies. So Joe and I saw June as thirty days of purgatory, the month of endless and meaningless projects. One summer when we lived in New Jersey, on the first day of our father's vacation, we arrived home from school to his instructions to remove all the rocks from our nearly barren backyard. I protested, reminding my father that he had grown up on narrow, concrete streets in Philadelphia in a brick row home with no backyard. What did he know about lawn management?

Before my father could reach me with his outstretched right hand, Joe stepped between us and ushered me out the back door. "No problem. Got it, Dad." Joe grabbed the back of my shirt and pulled me in the direction of the backyard, where we put on a show for our father who watched from the backdoor as we picked up rocks, one at a time, and threw each one into the woods behind our house.

While I accompanied each throw with a complaint, Joe calmly explained his strategy: "Make it look like we're busy. Dad's already stir-crazy with nothing to do. He'll disappear into the garage or the attic in a couple of minutes, and we can disappear too." Sure enough, within five minutes our father left in search of something else to do around the house. Joe and I walked into the woods and spent the rest of the afternoon climbing trees and laughing that we looked sufficiently dirty to pass for doing yard work.

Now, as I stepped from our car into the August humidity, my cotton T-shirt clung to dollops of sweat on my chest and back as I helped Joe carry his luggage to the curbside check-in at the Fort Lauderdale airport.

"All the way through to Tulsa. Connection in Atlanta," Joe said to the skycap. He put two suitcases on the curb.

"You can't leave this car parked here," someone said from behind me.

I turned and saw an overweight cop standing next to my car, his hands parked on his hips.

"He's just helping me drop off my bags, officer," Joe said. "He's not staying."

"Not unless he wants a ticket," the cop said.

"Get going, bro. You can't afford a ticket," Joe said. He grinned and added, "And you sure can't afford to tell Dad you got one."

"Today, son. I got traffic piling up," the cop said.

I handed Joe's third bag to the skycap. Then I glanced at the cop. He

The Best Player
I Ever Coached

By JORDAN OLIVAR
Yale University

A PHILADELPHIA sports writer once wrote: "There has probably been no player in Villanova history as consistently great and yet so unspectacular as John Sandusky."

It is all a matter of viewpoint, for to me any tackle who can regularly pull out of the line, get around the defensive and lead the interference is spectacular. Sandusky, six feet one and 260 pounds,

was tremendously agile for such a chunky man. He used his agility and massive physique to become one of the finest blockers I ever saw, on the line or in the open, during the three years 1946–47–48 that I coached him at Villanova.

On a punt return against Georgetown, our ball carrier shook off one tackler, but seemed to be trapped by two more. Sandusky, moving in like a giant scythe, cut down both men with a single mighty block and set up a sixty-yard run. Memorable as it is, that feat was only typical.

Sandusky was one of the few players I ever saw who actually looked forward with pleasure to wind sprints in training. Proud of his speed, the big man frequently put loafing halfbacks to shame. He was "big" mentally as well as physically, for he called blocking signals on the line and could come out of the game with unerring information on the defenses used against us and the adjustments made against our flankers and spreads.

In the days of the two-platoon system, Sandusky played practically all the way in every game. He was a first-stringer from his start as a freshman at Villanova and still is in this, his fifth season with the Cleveland Browns.

VILLANOVA UNIVERSITY
Sandusky . . . like a giant scythe.

Article on former Villanova offensive lineman John Sandusky written by his college coach, Jordan Oliver.

John and Ruth Sandusky on their wedding day, Philadelphia, 1950.

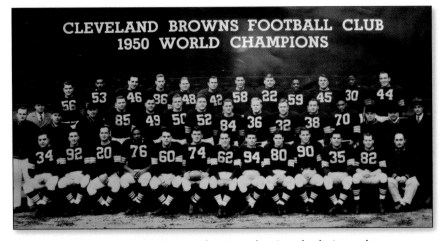

Cleveland Browns, 1950 team photo; John Sandusky's rookie season.
John, middle row, fifth from left, wearing number 49.

John Sandusky's 1953 Cleveland Browns team photo.
He is now wearing number 78.

Ruth and John Sandusky with sons Jim (left) and Jack in Cleveland, 1955.

The Baltimore Colts 1964 coaching staff. *Front*: Don Shula;
back, left to right: Chuck Knoll, Bill Arnsparger, Dick Bielski,
Charlie Winner, John Sandusky, and Don McCafferty.

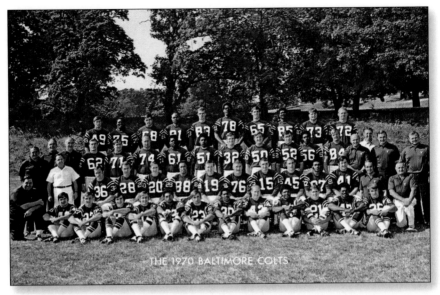

1970 Baltimore Colts team photo. John Sandusky, lower left, front row.

Gerry Sandusky (*far right*), a 13-year-old Philadelphia Eagles ball boy on the sidelines at Veteran's Stadium in Philadelphia, 1973.

John Sandusky and wife, Ruth,
at their Cooper City, Florida home, circa 1980.

Gerry Sandusky interviewing John Sandusky in the Miami Dolphins
locker room, September 1986.

John Sandusky, with his sons as groomsmen,
at his wedding to Shirley Petty, June 1987.

John Sandusky singing at a fundraiser for a scholarship foundation
honoring his late son, Joe, March 2000.

John Sandusky with grandson Zack, June 2001.

Back, left to right: Gerry, Lee Ann, and John Sandusky;
front: Katy, and Zack Sandusky, November 2004.

Zack Sandusky at the graves of his grandparents, John and Ruth Sandusky and his uncle, Joe Sandusky, Easter Sunday 2007.

Gerry Sandusky interviewing Baltimore Ravens head coach John Harbaugh prior to Super Bowl XLVII, at the New Orleans Superdome, February 3, 2013.

was looking at my license plate and pulling out his ticket pad. "Have a great season, bro," I said.

"Move it now, or you've got a ticket, kid."

I slipped behind the steering wheel of our parents' Plymouth Volare without a word of protest or a last good-bye.

As I pulled into the stream of traffic I glanced in my rearview mirror and saw the outline of Joe's dark brown hair and broad back as he walked into the terminal.

I never saw him again.

A month later the crowd of high school students, neighbors, and football players had slowly, silently slipped away from the cemetery following the burial service. Grief had already divided my mother and father. My mom stood at one end of Joe's coffin, my father at the other end. My brothers, sister, and I stood in between them, each of us with a hand on Joe's oak coffin, my thoughts a knotted braid of memories and regrets. Tears streamed down my face as I fell deeper into the black hole of mourning. Who do you turn to for answers when the person who had them all is gone? Don Shula had sought me out in the back of the church before the funeral and told me to be strong, be strong for my parents. How do you do that when you weren't the strong one to begin with? I just nodded. What I needed was to hear Joe's voice, that thick, calm voice as broad as his shoulders, as deep as his chest—a voice gone forever. How could I be strong for my parents? What did I know about strength? I knew about playing basketball, cracking jokes, English class. I knew about picking up sweaty jerseys and folding clean towels. I knew about avoiding my father three days before a big game.

The only strength I knew about I had borrowed from Joe. The summer before, he started to teach me how to lift weights. He took me to Gold's Gym in Hollywood, a long, narrow building with a concrete pad for a floor and round lights, the kind police use in criminal interrogations in the movies, hanging from a black grid of metal pipes in the unfinished ceiling. A rack of dumbbells lined one wall. Mirrors lined the other wall.

Joe's strength and body had expanded since he started playing college football. He had powerful muscles that ran in the shape of a V from his waist to his shoulders, chiseled like Michelangelo's *David*. The muscles in his chest, arms, and long legs were strong and powerful like an oak compared to my physique of a weed. He wanted to show me how to change that. We started with the bench press. Joe lifted 320 pounds with the ease of doing pushups. When my turn came he stripped the weights from the 45-pound bar. "Start with this," he said. Just then a weightlifter wearing bright orange shorts and a too-tight-fitting tank top walked over to us, his swollen chest and shoulder muscles glistening with sweat. The body-builders protested. "Hey, don't take all the weight off the bar," he said. "House rules. You can't lift it with weights on the bar, you find another gym. Got it?"

I felt like a slug he had sprinkled salt on, shriveling where I stood. "Let's just leave, Joe," I pleaded. Joe ignored me. He walked up to the weightlifter, stood in his personal space, and looked down on him. Joe's nostrils flared as he said, "He'll lift what I say he'll lift. And don't talk to my brother again, because one day he'll be strong enough to kick your ass. Until then I'll do it for him if you say another word." We worked out for the next hour uninterrupted, despite my inability to lift anything heavier than the bar, a bar that felt as awkward and foreign that day as his casket felt now.

The doctor said something called sepsis had killed Joe. It was an infection that snuck into his body through a cyst caused by his shoulder pads. That didn't mean anything to me. They were just words, an inept explanation of why the smooth, polished wood where I rested my hand had to come into our lives. Lifting my hand from the lid of Joe's coffin would mean saying good-bye forever. My father's hand spread out next to mine. It looked soldered to the coffin. The sound of my sobs vanished behind something I had never heard before—his tears. A sound of agony bubbled up from deep inside his heaving chest, the sound of a tiger chuffing. Disbelief. Crushing pain. I wanted to reach out and hug my father, tell him everything would be all right, have him do the same for me. But I couldn't. Neither could he. I knew from the pain twisting across his face that even if we hugged right now, it would bring us both more pain because we would both wish we were hugging Joe.

After Joe's death my father retreated to the only place where he could substitute familiarity for comfort: football. He worked even longer hours. My mother visited Joe's grave every day. The three of us went to the cemetery on Sunday mornings after mass, before we left for the stadium. Even standing at Joe's grave, my father didn't talk about Joe. We stood there silently, staring at the proof of our pain, a brass grave marker with Joe's name on it and his all-too-brief life span: 1959–1978. When we returned to the car, if we talked at all, my father usually stumbled through the conversation on unsure footing. Even his reprimands had lost their power of certainty. The sight of our uncut grass as we pulled out of our driveway on the way to church had triggered a rebuke. "I thought I asked you . . ." my father said, his words prickly but fading into an indiscernible mumble.

"I'll get to it tomorrow," I said.

"He's hurting too, John," my mother whispered while looking out the passenger window at our empty house. My father clamped his lips together, perhaps suspecting I didn't need more to feel bitter or angry about.

I left for college the following year, attending Towson University in Baltimore, where, after one season of sitting on the bench, my withered self-perception as a basketball player led me to try the one thing I knew I could talk to my father about: playing football.

When I told him during my spring break about my idea of trying out for the football team, he raised his eyebrows and grinned. "You have some catching up to do, but you're a good enough athlete," he said. I had forgotten what his smile looked like.

The following summer I worked out in the Dolphins' weight room with players, played catch with Mike Shula in the afternoon, and, when my father had time, asked him to show me the finer points of blocking.

Two weeks before training camp began, Don Strock and several of the Dolphins players took part in voluntary workouts on the practice field. I watched from the open-air weight room next to the field. My father had stopped by during his lunch break to see me.

Strock called over to me: "We're short a tight end. Come help out."

I looked at my father. "He's calling you, not me," he said.

"But I . . . I mean . . . I'm not . . ."

"Nobody ever improved just talking about it," my dad said, nodding in the direction of the practice field.

So out I went.

Strock and twelve other Dolphins wearing aqua shorts, white T-shirts, and cleats were playing seven-on-seven. Seven offensive players against seven defensive players, passing offense against passing defense. I stepped into the offensive huddle and looked to Strock for a quick tutorial after he called a play that meant nothing to me. "Run five yards upfield. Cut over the middle," Strock whispered.

As I lined up in my three-point stance at the line of scrimmage, the fingertips of my right hand pressed against the Bermuda grass, my feet staggered, Dolphins safety Mike Kozlowski stood across the line from me in a crouch. Kozlowski had chiseled biceps that stretched his tight-fitting shirt. Strock shouted "hut," and I attempted to come out of my stance exactly how my father had shown me, knowing he was watching from the weight room, and I felt the full force of Kozlowski's forearm slam into my chest, sending me backward onto my butt three yards behind the line.

On the next play Kozlowski threw me face first into the grass. On the third play he smacked me in the shoulder, sending me tumbling into Strock's feet. I looked up to see my father walking away from the weight room and Don Shula waiting for me in the huddle, his jaw jutting out, eyes ignited.

"You're screwing up the drill," Shula said. "Get off the goddamn line and run the route. Otherwise, why in the hell are you out here?"

"Coach, I was just working out. Strock said . . ."

"I don't give a goddamn what Strock said. You're out here, now act like you belong." Then Shula bent over in a three-point stance and showed me how to drive off my right foot, keep my shoulders low and parallel to the ground, and push free of Kozlowski at the line.

The next play, with Kozlowski staring in my eyes and the heat of Coach Shula's glare on the back of my head, I wrestled my way past the Dolphins safety, ran a short route, and caught a pass from Strock.

I must have had too big of a smile when I returned to the huddle. "It was a five-yard gain. Stop acting like you won the damn Super Bowl," Shula said, vanquishing my grin. "This time Kozlowski is going to try to jam you on the inside because of your last move, so . . ." And he showed me another technique that worked perfectly. For the next forty-five minutes I did everything Coach Shula told me. I played like I belonged. My fear of getting yelled at by Coach Shula after each play overrode my fear of getting hit by Mike Kozlowski at the start of each play. No one would confuse me with an NFL prospect, but for close to an hour I played at a level I could have never imagined. On the final play of the workout Strock threw a pass to me that I caught in the back of the end zone. I tried to conceal my excitement, as though every afternoon of my life I caught a touchdown pass from an NFL quarterback, but as I looked back toward the field I saw Coach Shula had already left and missed the play. As I walked back to the locker room with Strock, drenched in sweat and smiling, I felt a tug of disappointment that my father hadn't stayed long enough to see my best performance on a football field in my life. The next month in a scrimmage at Towson I broke my right leg and ankle, an injury that ended my brief football career without me collecting a single statistic or a single smile from my father.

The end of college brought me back to South Florida and back home for the same temptation that often lures twenty-one-year-olds back to their high school bedroom: free rent. I started my broadcasting career at a Miami TV station, WSVN, as an unpaid intern. As I progressed to a producer then a reporter covering the Miami Dolphins, I saw my father more at work than at home, and I saw two different men.

Free rent came at a price. Six years removed, the pain of Joe's death had frozen my parents' house in a time warp, a place where the feeling of loss shadowed each of us. It had the musty, airless feel of a mausoleum. Nothing had changed in my brother's room. His clothes hung in the closet the way he left them on the day I drove him to the airport. A wallet, leather keychain, hairbrush, and pens sat on his desk, frozen in time, unmoved since they returned from Tulsa in a cardboard box containing his belongings, memories now trapped in emotional amber. My father had encouraged me to stay at home, selling me on the benefits of banking my paycheck and the hope of bringing a spark back to the house.

"You'll give your mother someone to talk to," he confided. "She doesn't talk to me, and I don't know what to say to her," he said over lunch in the Dolphins' team cafeteria. He knew how to diagram a tackle trap or a fold block for any defense his offensive line might face, but he couldn't diagram a way out of the emotional sinkhole that had swallowed our family and his relationship with my mother.

During the day I covered practice at the Dolphins' facility, where I usually found my father with a smile on his face, happy to see me, willing to make time to talk after practice, asking me how my job was going, what I had learned that week, who my photographer was, how my interviews went that day. He had taken an interest in my life that I had never seen before. But at home he stewed in silence, sitting in his lounge chair in the evening watching TV, *Monday Night Football, Magnum, P.I.,* or *Cheers* while my mother either sat on the sofa and repaired an old dress with a needle and thread or sat in front of her sewing machine in the dining room making baptismal bibs for the church. The whirring of the sewing machine's engine and the glottal vibrations of my father's snoring were the only sounds passing between my parents.

Before long the current of the season captured both of us—but not my mother—in its wake. The Dolphins had started the season with a 4–0 record. Dolphins quarterback Dan Marino had South Floridians whispering hopes of another perfect season. By late October a win against Buffalo had pushed the Dolphins' record to 9–0. Marino looked unstoppable. Super Bowl hopes swirled through the sell-out crowds at the Orange Bowl. 10–0. 11–0. The Dolphins' season took on the giddy, runaway feeling of destiny for many people, but not for my mother.

Her daily routine would start at Winn Dixie, the grocery store two miles from our house, to buy fresh flowers for her visit to Joe's grave. She would return home to do laundry, clean, cook, and sew, all with her dog, Dixie, a stray she had found the year before outside the grocery store, by her side. Mom had lost weight since Joe died. Her skin and muscles hung from her shoulders and arms like linen drying on a clothesline. The small lines by her eyes that had appeared when she smiled now were a permanent reminder of age and sorrow. The red housedress she wore on her daily errands hung loosely on her. She wore her graying hair pulled back and held in place with a bandana. She had no desire to buy new dresses, ones that fit better. They held no more interest to her than the Dolphins' 11–0 record.

A loss to San Diego in November spoiled the hopes of another Dolphins perfect season, but the guarantee of a playoff trip extended the work hours for my father and me, our paths crossing each day at Dolphins camp or Sunday mornings at church before home games.

The Catholic Mass hadn't changed since we buried Joe, but the impact of it had, at least for me. We still attended the same church, St. Bernadette's, a simple peak-roofed church with beige stucco walls. And my father still believed every word uttered from the pulpit. He took the gospel as, well, gospel truth. My mother did not.

The prayers of the faithful and readings from the New Testament now prompted questions from my mother on the car ride to Joe's grave. "If the kingdom of God is within, why do I feel so much pain inside?" she asked to no one in particular as my father pulled his car through the wrought-iron gates at the front of the cemetery.

My father gave her the look I remembered him flashing at me once when I couldn't figure out how to find a Phillips-head screwdriver. "That's why they call it faith, I suppose," he said. He had taken the path of more. More belief. More singing during mass—the louder the better. More volunteering. Sure, I'll help collect the money, hand out pamphlets. Religion was something to do, follow the leader, fill the void. Catholic was a verb to my father, just like manhood. I had learned that a few summers before at training camp.

The Dolphins had signed Thomas "Hollywood" Henderson as a free agent. A former star linebacker with the Dallas Cowboys, Henderson had a gold front tooth. He finished conversations with a wink.

The Dolphins' equipment manager, Dan Dowd, couldn't stand players who acted like stars.

During one muggy August afternoon practice Henderson sprinted from the field in the middle of the workout to use the toilet in the locker room. I was in the locker room filling a tub of Gatorade. Henderson handed me his helmet as he ran by. "Hold that," he said.

Dan Dowd grinned. "Got him now. Hand that to me."

Using a wooden tongue depressor, Dan glopped Vaseline into the shell of Henderson's helmet. Then he poured in baby powder. Dan returned the helmet in time for me to hand it to Henderson as he ran through the locker room. Back on the field, Henderson tugged on his helmet, setting off a small mushroom cloud of white powder from his facemask while Vaseline oozed down his face.

Players and coaches broke into laughter, even Coach Shula. Henderson pivoted toward me as I returned to the field carrying the cooler of Gatorade. He pointed at me, shaking his head, flashing his gold tooth.

In the locker room, after practice, Henderson tossed his helmet to me and shouted in a showman's voice, "Hey funny man, clean my helmet."

I tossed it back. "Clean it yourself. I didn't do anything to it."

Ohhs and ahhs sang through the locker room as Henderson rose from the stool in front of his locker and walked up to me. I had nowhere to go. If I ran, I would never live it down. If I got into a fight with a player, my father and Coach Shula would kill me.

Henderson smiled. Then in a flash of quickness I could barely follow, he darted toward me, wrapped his arms around my waist, lifted me off my feet, and slammed me into a locker. Despite the pain radiating from the middle of my back, I lowered my right shoulder and drove it under Henderson's ribs, knocking him off balance.

Players gathered around us in a loose circle.

Henderson had established the rules without saying a word. I understood. No punches. Only clean moves. Nothing dirty.

My heart pounded as he came at me a second time, knocking me off my feet. He pounced on me. I used his momentum to roll on top of him. I could hear cheers and hollers around us. He quickly flipped me. Then the locker room fell silent.

"What the hell is going on here?" Shula bellowed.

"Just a little horseplay, Coach. All friendly," Hollywood assured him. He flashed Shula a smile and winked as he unwrapped his right arm from around my head.

That night in our dorm room, as my father reached over to turn out the light, he said, "Shula told me you hung in there with Henderson when you could've gotten your ass kicked."

Before I could respond, my father clicked off the light. To him, manhood was a statement, an action, not a conversation.

He saw Catholicism the same way.

My mother did not. To her, religion—and manhood for that matter—had become a question mark.

Standing at Joe's grave, I wanted to ask my father whether he really thought Joe sat on a cloud somewhere with Saint Peter and Jesus? And if he didn't know any more than any priest, any more than his own sister who was a nun, where Joe was, then how could he go along with all of those words about the Body of Christ, the Lamb of God, the Apostles' Creed that priests spit out as predictably as a vending machine? But he did. And he sang louder than everyone else at church to prove it. The more my mother challenged religion, the louder he sang. The more she pondered, the less he talked. I offered nothing, siding more with my mother but mostly wanting to get back in the car and drive away from the awkwardness of Sunday mornings.

The Dolphins sailed through the regular season to a 14–2 record. Marino threw for more than five thousand yards while my father's offensive line surrendered the fewest sacks in the NFL. As the playoffs began, and Marino's star rose, so did my father's. More and more often he showed up on sideline shots during national TV broadcasts standing next to Shula, prompting announcers to point out that John Sandusky's offensive line had become the best in the NFL, along with Miami's amazing young quarterback.

Wins over Seattle and Pittsburgh in the playoffs sent the Dolphins back to the Super Bowl to face the San Francisco 49ers.

Two years earlier, in Super Bowl XVII, the Dolphins had lost to the Washington Redskins in a game they had led until midway through the fourth quarter. This time, however, the Dolphins had Dan Marino. In a season when nearly everything had gone right, what could possibly go wrong now?

My television station had sent so many people to the West Coast to cover the Super Bowl that it didn't have enough staff left in Miami to anchor all the shows. The news director, Dave Choate, who ran the newsroom, scheduled me to anchor my first show, the six o'clock sportscast on Super Bowl Sunday. I saw it as the chance of a lifetime. He understood the lack of downside. Even if I flopped, no one would notice. I worked for an NBC affiliate, and that year the Super Bowl was on ABC. Everyone in Miami would be watching the Super Bowl. Everyone. Dave Choate told me even he didn't plan on watching me, at least not live.

Throughout the week I called my parents and talked with my father about the game, his concerns, Marino, and the 49ers quarterback, Joe

Montana. My father sounded energized but concerned. He had lost two Super Bowls and knew how quickly plans for celebration could spoil. He frequently turned the conversation back in my direction.

"How are your preparations going?" he asked. "Ready for Sunday?"

And I heard a long-forgotten ring of excitement in my mother's voice. "Quite the day coming up for my boys," she said. "You'll do great." Her warmth calmed my jangled nerves.

On Super Bowl Sunday I called my parents to wish them good luck. My voice must have betrayed my emotions, runaway roots of worry and doubt twisting around my lungs, squeezing air out of me before dropping in my stomach, undigested panic.

"You sound a little tense," my dad said.

"I expected to say that to you," I said, forcing a laugh.

"I get that way too. It's like you want to crawl back to bed and avoid the thing you've been working for your entire life. But you'll do it. You'll do great. I can't wait to hear about it after the game."

He understood.

In our newsroom I watched the Dolphins take an early lead on a field goal. Then a Marino touchdown pass late in the first quarter gave Miami a 10–7 edge as a late afternoon fog rolled through Stanford Stadium, and I walked into the TV studio in Miami to anchor my first sportscast.

Even the news anchors were watching the game on a monitor in the studio.

I sat at the anchor desk during the commercial break before the sportscast and listened to play-by-play announcer Frank Gifford talk about the Dolphins' pass protection while a camera caught a glimpse of my father on the sidelines, his scowl and glare cutting through the Bay Area mist.

The floor director said, "stand by." My heart hammered against my chest. The red talent light above the middle camera in the TV studio turned on, and the news anchor, Rick Sanchez, who would later make some controversial remarks on CNN, welcomed me to the anchor desk.

I smiled and turned to my camera, ready to read the script I had written and placed in the teleprompter.

A blank lens stared back at me.

The teleprompter had broken. A rain forest of perspiration rose from my skin, soaking the dress shirt beneath my blue suit coat.

"Start of the second quarter in Super Bowl Nineteen at Stanford Stadium. Right now the Dolphins have a ten-seven lead," I heard a voice say. It was my voice. I could feel words passing across my lips, but with my eyes locked onto the blank TV camera, I felt like I was still a viewer, watching someone else talk on television, someone who looked very nervous and very wet.

Five minutes later I finished anchoring my first sportscast. Sweat had dampened my shirt, and my hopes of sharing a perfect day with my father began to evaporate as the 49ers quarterback came to life. Joe Montana had thrown his first touchdown pass, and the 49ers had taken the lead, one they would never surrender. The 49ers went on to beat Miami 38–16, my father's third Super Bowl loss.

My day hadn't gone much better than my father's except for one detail: no one had seen my struggles. The entire world had seen his.

On the phone that night my dad sounded exhausted but oddly relieved and also excited for me. The buildup, pressure, expectation of a Super Bowl had passed. But my career as a broadcaster had begun. Both of my parents sounded thrilled. We spent the conversation talking about a sportscast no one even saw, as though that somehow equaled the Super Bowl in importance and interest. To my parents it did.

When I tried to turn the conversation back to the game, my dad shrugged off his disappointment. "We've handled bigger losses before. We'll handle this one too."

I believed him, without knowing another loss loomed, one none of us could imagine.

— Chapter Seven —

COACHING ALONE

Despite losing the Super Bowl the season before, my father seemed to have found his footing again. He laughed with his players in practice. He invited friends and neighbors over to sit around the pool, drink Manhattans, and let an evening evolve into laughter, storytelling, and singing. And he could sing. His renditions of "Danny Boy" and other ballads sounded like John McDermott and the Irish Tenors singing in our backyard. He had become what my brothers, sister, and I had long called him behind his back: Big John. A big man, a big voice, a big presence. Now, as adults, we no longer hid our nickname from him, and he seemed as comfortable with me calling him Big John as Dad. His comfort level did not, however, last for long.

No sooner had the Dolphins run their record to 4–1 at the start of the 1985 season with a win over Pittsburgh when trouble resurfaced at home. Mom, in an effort to find her own way back to life, had quit smoking following the Super Bowl. It seemed to backfire. She lost weight and energy. Her desire to eat, already minimal for the past seven years, seemed to vanish. On weekends I noticed she would retreat to her bedroom for long naps.

In the years since Joe's death the weight of grief had pulled on my mother. She had a perpetual look of exhaustion, bags beneath her eyes, skin sagging across her delicate jaw line.

A visit to the family doctor raised further concern. He wanted her to check in to the hospital for testing immediately. My mother didn't want me to worry. "The hospital is less than a mile from the cemetery," she said. She measured everything by the distance from Joe's grave. Close was good.

Dad and I visited her every day before or after work. Doctors diagnosed her with having a failing gall bladder, and a day after surgery they called her operation successful. Mom told Dad not to worry and sent him out of town for his game in New York. The Dolphins lost to the Jets. A day after my father returned I saw him in the kitchen pouring his first cup of coffee. He was biting on the inside corner of his lip, running his hand along the morning stubble on his cheeks. He couldn't put his worry into words, but I could tell he sensed something was wrong.

Early in her hospital stay my mom would ask me at length about my job. She seemed far less amazed than me that a TV station would let me do interviews and produce stories for the news or that my part-time job as an editor and a production assistant had evolved into a full-time job as a producer and sports reporter. "Good interview yesterday with the bowler. Seemed like a nice man," she would say.

She had lost more weight since her surgery. A three-day recovery in the hospital became a week. Then two. My interviews with bowlers or golfers or tennis players or the live report I did from a boxing match on Miami Beach seemed to bring fewer smiles from and shorter conversations with my mother. The Dolphins lost three out of four games. Their season looked on the brink of collapse. So did my mother. Her hospital stay had grown to a month.

In the evenings I would sit with my father in my mom's hospital room, tension growing by the day. A waxy sheen had slipped across her face. I couldn't tell whether it was illness or the fluorescent lights that gave her sagging skin a greenish tint. Her food tray looked untouched, with applesauce, chicken, a slice of white bread languishing on plastic the way she languished on white hospital sheets. Doctors had no answers, and my parents had no conversations. Frequently my mom slept, or tried to, opening her eyes to let my father know she would prefer he not tap his fingers on the metal bars next to her bed while he stared out through the venetian blinds that looked onto University Boulevard, the busy four-lane road adjacent to the hospital. At the end of visiting hours my father and

I walked to the parking lot. I wanted to push him to demand answers. Call in experts. Get second opinions. Third opinions. Do something. Do anything.

The one time I gathered the courage to try, he cut me off. We stood in the nearly empty parking lot, in the soft yellow glow of the low-pressure sodium-vapor street lamp above his car, backlighting him as he pointed his right index finger at me, punctuating his words, a silhouette of anger: "Doctors know what they're doing. They're doing their best." His chest roiled, air moving in and out of it too quickly, almost convulsively. "They'll tell us if there's something else we should do," he said. "They will tell us," he repeated, emphasizing each word with an equal, anchored weight. "They. Will. Tell. Us." He listened to higher authorities, so why couldn't I? Doctors, priests, nuns—all beyond reproach or question. He slammed his car door shut. Topic closed. He drove away, leaving me standing alone, the cone of yellow light falling in an empty circle in front of me, empty of answers or direction.

I wanted to push him more. But I lacked the courage to lean any further into a volcano.

Ruth Ann, who now lived in New Jersey with her husband, Bob, and seven-year-old daughter, Kristen, called for regular updates on Mom and Dad. I could hear the frustration seeping into her voice, a voice that tried to coax timelines, medications, examination results from me, results I didn't have to give her. Ruth was a patient listener, but she was also a woman who had to keep a running clock in her head along with a calendar of streaming events: preschool for Kristen, tumbling after school, pick up Bob's two kids from his first marriage for their winter break, get home in time to get ready for a work event at Bob's office, find another babysitter when her regular girl called in sick.

"Gerry," she said, her tone now a little more terse, clipped, "what is Dad doing about the doctors doing nothing?" she asked.

Now I felt my loyalties tested. Mom had always made the connections in the family, telling everyone that Jack was getting a divorce from

Ginger, or Jim was changing jobs and leaving UPS, or Ruth and Bob were going to close the restaurant they had opened. Mom was the one who always knew what to say and when to say it. I didn't. I didn't agree with my father's approach, but I was the only one who saw his struggles every day, the only one who heard the weight of doubt and sadness plunk at his voice like uncertain fingers striking an out-of-tune piano. I might challenge him, but I felt disloyal criticizing him. I didn't know what to tell my sister. I settled for a careful landing space: "He's doing his best."

"His best what?"

"Ruth, I think Mom is . . ."

I heard the sound of glass breaking and Kristen crying in the background. "I have to go," Ruth said.

The following week Jim, now married and still living in Baltimore, flew into Fort Lauderdale. I picked him up at the airport, and we drove to the hospital. He still had a square-shouldered certainty from his time a decade and a half before as a college linebacker. He had muscular arms, a thick chest, and a way of expressing his frustration exactly like our father, by pulling his lips into a taut O-shape that quivered before he let words escape his mouth.

His visit brightened Mom's mood. She delighted in the photos Jim spread out on her bed of his three-year-old son, Luke, and infant daughter, Sarah. Mom lifted each photo, knuckles protruding on her emaciated hands as she kissed each picture as gently as though she were tucking her grandchildren into bed. Jim stroked Mom's hair and pushed a lie past the smile he forced. "You look good, Mom. We just have to get you a little stronger so we can get you home."

Mom didn't respond.

A day before Jim left, Ruth Ann arrived. At the hospital she freshened a flower arrangement on the nightstand in Mom's room. Ruth Ann stood at the foot of Mom's bed, shifting her weight to her right hip as though she were resting a child there. She smiled and said, "Would you like us to bring you some food? You don't seem to be eating much of what they give you here."

Mom said no. She didn't have much of an appetite. But thanks. Just seeing her kids was good enough for her. Sorry Jack couldn't get down this week. But glad he's working. Bricklayers have to work when they can in December in Baltimore. Mom told Ruth Ann how much she liked what she had done with her auburn-colored hair, and Ruth Ann fielded the compliment with a smile that did little to hide the worry pouring from her dark brown eyes as she sat on the edge of Mom's bed and pulled photos of Kristen and Bob from her purse.

Back at the house Jim, Ruth Ann, and I settled around cold beers at the kitchen table. Jim's gentleness disappeared, replaced by what seemed like a reprimand for my not managing everything better.

"Mom's giving up. She's just giving up," Jim said to Ruth Ann. "And he's letting her," he added, pointing his index finger at me. "And Dad needs to be more aggressive with everyone. Mom, the doctors, everyone."

"Hold on," Ruth Ann interjected. "It's not his fault." She peered at me above the tops of her glasses before turning her attention back to Jim and added, "I'd do some things differently, but he's not in charge. And Dad doesn't have Mom to make all the decisions. He has to make them."

"Guys, I'm actually here," I said, walking to the refrigerator to grab another beer.

Jim had practically raised me in college. He and his wife, Garf, moved from Annapolis to Towson when I went to Towson University to help look out for me, knowing I might veer off course after Joe died. He still had the build of a linebacker—broad shoulders, thin waist. He still stuck out his chest as though ready to absorb a running back's block.

When Dad came home from work that night Ruth and Jim could see the fatigue leeching color from his cheeks, so they let the conversation drift without harsh edges. Their overlapping visits went by with a tidal surge and retreat of concern and blame before their own lives and families took them back to New Jersey and Baltimore. When I dropped Jim off at the airport he gave me a hug then looked me in the eyes. He leaned in to me, his eyes drawn into a squint. "Don't let Mom quit like this, and get Dad focused," he said, insinuating I was an accomplice in Mom's demise and Dad's uncertainty.

A three-game win streak resuscitated the Dolphins' season, but not my mother. The latest tests showed a spot on her lung. She was too weak for more surgery.

In the first week of December the Dolphins faced the undefeated Chicago Bears on Monday Night Football. The Bears had a 13–0 record. If the Bears could get past Miami, they would almost certainly become the first team to go through an NFL season undefeated since the 1972 Dolphins.

On the day of the game Dad and I visited Mom in the hospital in the early afternoon before we headed to the Orange Bowl. Mom had little to say. I held her right hand. My father held her left. The three of us sat in the antiseptic room staring at the random speckles on the tile floor, the rectangular, geometric grid of the drop ceiling, the soap opera on the TV hanging from the ceiling in the corner of the room. I watched my parents stare at everything but each other, everything but the end of their time together.

Earlier in the week, on one of my visits before going to the TV station, a visit that didn't overlap with my father's, my mom and I had a long conversation, the kind that begins innocently enough, talking about mundane things, laundry, tourist traffic, grocery shopping, the Bears game, a live report I would get to do from the Orange Bowl—my biggest TV assignment so far. She promised to watch. Then, like sediment settling in a slow-moving creek, our conversation found a depth, a stillness that drew my attention along with the topic deeper and deeper. Even the din of traffic from University Boulevard fell away, along with all pretense of healing.

"Sweetie, I know I'm dying. And that's okay," she said, free from anxiety. Dying wasn't a bad thing. She was going to see Joe, a trip she wanted to make. I sat and listened, tumbling through the thought of losing her. I was twenty-four, my career just starting. I was coming to life, and she was saying good-bye.

As rivulets of tears worked down my cheeks, she ran her frail hand across my forearm, compounding my sense of helplessness. She was dying, and I needed comfort.

"I wouldn't have done much of a job as a mom if my son couldn't cry for me when I was dying, now would I?" she said, her frail, tired smile trying to lift guilt from my sadness.

When I asked her why she hadn't had that kind of talk with Dad, she exhaled slowly, searching for the right words. "We haven't talked about much since Joe died. Certainly not about Joe. He doesn't know how. It's easier to avoid than engage." She stopped and smiled at me, her soft brown eyes letting me know she wasn't mad. She didn't want me to take sides or intervene. She just wanted me to understand. "Over the years I've learned to wait until the off-season to talk about anything important with your father. He doesn't hear much during the season, certainly not this week with the Bears game." She added the smallest laugh, lightening the mood.

As I wiped away tears, she added, "He's going to need you now. You'll need each other."

The Dolphins beat the Bears 38–24. The next morning Dad took the game ball to the hospital like a high school football star beaming to see his girlfriend. The nurses he passed in the stark white hallways congratulated him on the win. A Dolphins coach who makes daily visits to a hospital becomes a hallway celebrity.

He showed Mom the game ball. Here it was, *the* ball from *the* game. The game all of South Florida was talking about today. The team had sent the ball to her after the win, the biggest win of the year, the win that kept the Dolphins' place in NFL history secure as the only perfect team.

Mom glanced at the ball. Another football. She turned away.

The joy vanished from my father's face like the flash of a light bulb when it burns out. Darkness. Done.

Dad set the football on Mom's bedside table next to her tray of uneaten food and a cluster of get-well cards from well-wishers who didn't know how to say, "I'm sorry you're dying so young. It doesn't seem fair." Dad didn't know how to say it either. He had hoped the football would say it for him.

My mom died on a Sunday, ten days before Christmas.

The next night the Dolphins played on Monday Night Football again. This time Dad didn't stand on the sidelines, and I didn't do a live report from the field or sit in the press box. We sat together in our living room after a day of making funeral plans and watched the game on TV as the Dolphins played the Patriots at the Orange Bowl.

Midway through the second quarter, during a break in the action, ABC broadcaster Al Michaels explained my father's conspicuous absence from the sideline, praising him as one of the top assistant coaches in the NFL and extending condolences for his loss. Michaels, the announcer who once asked all of America, "Do you believe in miracles? Yes!" when the United States shocked Russia in the hockey semifinals of the 1976 Olympics, a game I had watched with my father. Michaels had no miracles to offer that night.

Dad sat in his recliner in the living room. He had never missed a game, not since his rookie year with the Cleveland Browns in 1950. He had coached the week Joe died. This time the game played out without him. I sat on the sofa, watching my father as much as the game. We had grown used to an empty house over the past three months with Mom in the hospital. Now the emptiness had a permanence about it, a vague cloudiness highlighted by the voice of Monday Night Football announcer Al Michaels. It felt like Michaels had walked into our living room, looked us in the eyes, and spoke to us in a whispery wish-I-didn't-have-to-say-this tone of voice. He said elegantly what the doctors had bumbled through the day before: "We tried everything we could . . . she just wasn't strong enough . . . sometimes . . ." Al Michaels's words made it real for Dad: "At the far too young age of fifty-eight." Mom was gone.

Dad looked at me, a thin crescent of red around his eyes, his eyebrows raised, his lips pressed together. This time the silence didn't separate us. It joined us. Our family continued to shrink. It was just him and me now. Al Michaels's voice along with the game itself faded, replaced by the echo of my mother's words in her gentle voice, always more suited to a whisper than a shout: "He's going to need you now. You'll need each other."

My father retreated to his bedroom, the way he had the day the Colts fired him as their head coach, and he shut the door behind him as tightly as he had shut out his emotions over the past several weeks to face the void of coaching alone.

A month later the New England Patriots returned to the Orange Bowl and beat the Dolphins in the AFC Championship Game. And just like that, the football season ended, leaving my father to wrestle with his demon, a demon even Catholicism could not exorcise: the demon of free time.

Early in the off-season he settled into a routine of coming home from work and sitting in a yellow chair in the family room, a room he had rarely done more than walk through in the past, a chair I had never seen him sit in before. He gazed out at the pool, sometimes for minutes, sometimes for hours, each time as though it might hold the answers to questions he couldn't quite form.

"I can't get my head wrapped around it turning out this way," he said to me one evening, as the day's last sunlight slipped from the sky in a coral and turquoise sunset. I sat at the kitchen table, eating a slice of day-old pizza, listening, letting him talk. "We both figured I would die first, what with my weight and job stress," he said, his gaze fixed on the pool, his words soft enough to float on the water's surface. "Never occurred to me Mom might go first. Never. Or we wouldn't make it to retirement." He paused, stroking the back of Mom's dog Dixie, who stood only midway up his shin, a white and brown mix breed with a brown patch of fur that surrounded her left eye, then added, "together." He looked around the room that my mother had sponge painted a few years earlier a sunny, summer yellow, a slow camera pan revealing the room to him for the first time. "How long have we had that sofa?" he asked, nodding toward the white Naugahyde couch against the far wall.

"Since we moved here."

That winter we both learned the extent of our limitations. We could both cook eggs. I could make spaghetti. That meant dinner fell to me. On Mondays, my day off, I would cook a couple of pounds of spaghetti, dump jars of sauce on it, and leave it on the stove. The two of us served ourselves from the oversized metal pot throughout the week. When we ran out of dog food, we fed Dixie spaghetti too. When we ran out of spaghetti, we ate dinner out and brought Dixie leftovers.

The days of home-cooked meals had ended. The smell of Mom's London broil filling the kitchen, with its au jus drizzled onto baked potatoes, or her broccoli casseroles with sliced mushrooms swimming in bubbling melted cheese had become memories we treasured every time one of us opened the refrigerator and stared at the sparse landscape: a few beers, a half-empty jar of Prego spaghetti sauce, leftovers from Chinese carry-out.

I saw a hopeless look in my father's eyes when he camped in front of the refrigerator, a stare as empty as the shelves in front of him, the refrigerator light falling across his six o'clock shadow now speckled with gray, highlighting lines that ran alongside his eyes and between his cheeks and mouth, timelines of worry.

"We need to start grocery shopping on a regular basis. Get some kind of a system going, a strategy," Dad said to me, moving his right hand in the air like he was diagramming a tackle trap block.

"Yeah," I said, "right after I teach you how to do laundry."

Dad laughed. "What do you think this is?" he asked, pulling out a round, plastic dish from the back of the refrigerator. It held what remained of a turkey sandwich, eroded by bite marks and covered with a thin layer of fuzzy green and white mold. "Probably shouldn't eat things that look like that, huh?"

"Sounds like our new strategy," I said.

We both laughed. We knew we weren't going to start grocery shopping on a regular basis. Dad hadn't seen the inside of a grocery store in years. We weren't going to update the furniture in the living room that had started looking tired. We weren't going to dust. We weren't going to use the oven. Not unless something—or someone—drastic happened.

Dan Sekanovich was not someone drastic. But he was someone important.

The Dolphins hired him as their new defensive line coach in February, a month after the '85 season ended. His wife and kids stayed behind in Atlanta to finish out the school year, so until they joined him in South Florida in the summer, Dan moved in with Dad, me, and Dixie. Bald, tall, and stoop shouldered, Dan was quick with a grin and happy to accept the offer of a cold beer. Dan called me "Roomie." He had no more cooking or domestic skills than my father or me, but he did have something we both had lost track of: optimism.

Despite lines that tugged down on the corners of his eyes, nose, and mouth, giving him a downcast look, Dan saw all the benefits of three men and a dog living together. We had few rules and no one to impress. Having Dan as our new roommate also helped my father absorb the long, lonely hours at home.

By March the Dolphins' running backs coach, Carl Tasseff, had become a regular around the pool on weekends with his wife, Lucy. Drinking scotch together, Dan, Carl, and my dad would sing Irish ballads and talk about next season. Weeknights became movie nights. By the time I got home from work, sometimes after midnight, depending on my schedule at the station, I would frequently find Dan and Dad in the living room, Dad on his lounge chair, Dan's long frame stretched out across the couch, as they watched John Wayne movies or black-and-white World War II classics.

"I know how it ends," I said, walking past the TV one night on my way to the empty kitchen that I checked nightly for a gift of food from a neighbor.

"How's that?" my dad asked.

"We win. Germany loses. Japan falls. Been there done that."

"Good one, Roomie," Dan said, smiling.

"Funny, asshole. Tell me about which war you fought in," my dad said.

"He's got you there, Roomie."

By May I had started to find glass dishes of lasagna, sausage and peppers, and chicken parmigiana on my late-night forays to the kitchen, food all credited to someone my father called "a friend from church." I found it odd he never mentioned his friend by name.

When I didn't have to work early on Sunday I still tried to go to church with my father even though we took away very different experiences from it. Mass seemed to bring him to life; it reminded me of death.

My father walked into church beaming, greeting ushers, the priest, and other churchgoers with the smile I suspect he shared with family and friends on the day he returned home to Philadelphia after serving in the army in World War II. Good-bye Germany; hello life. I felt more like a double agent behind enemy lines, knowing I didn't belong there but content to look like I did.

Each week we seemed to sit closer to the front of the church, as though the altar had a magnet drawing my father toward it. The closer we got, the more I could see images of my brother and my mother's caskets sitting there in the main aisle, with priests saying words that brought no relief to me. Now, months removed from my mother's death, I could see my father enjoyed people at church reaching out to him, taking his emotional temperature.

"John, how are you?" a short, gray-haired woman asked as we walked toward the front door of the church. Her skin had the look of leather from too much exposure in the South Florida sun.

"I'm doing good, Dolores," he answered with a big smile—too big. He held the door open for her, and after Dolores walked ahead of us, my father whispered to me that she had lost her husband five years ago. Car accident. Damn shame.

I started to see nearly everyone at church that way. A greeting, a smile, then a whisper from my father about their problems, their losses. He had joined a club of emotional pain. Catholic mass seemed to add to the pain. At least for me.

Readings from the Old Testament made ancient Israel seem like a place more dangerous than a back alley in Detroit. Readings from the New Testament made me wonder how my father took St. Paul seriously. My father listened to the readings of Paul's first letter to the Corinthians with the rapt attention of an altar boy. His eyes locked on the pulpit. "For it is written I will destroy the wisdom of the wise, and will bring to nothing the understanding of the prudent." Once, after mass, I asked my father, "Do you know where Corinth is?"

"What are you talking about?"

"Corinth. Paul's letter to the Corinthians. Do you know where Corinth is?"

"What the hell does that have to do with anything?"

I changed my angle. "Do you know St. Paul never actually met Jesus?" My mother and I used to have these kinds of conversations all the time, probing, challenging, forcing each other to think, to figure out what we did and didn't believe.

My father returned a long stare set with a clenched jaw, his head angled slightly forward, the Big John kind of look that let me know he didn't care whether St. Paul never met Jesus, but he might punch me if I continued with this line of questioning.

After the readings came the Responsorial Psalm. From the pulpit a member of the congregation read out prayers in a formulaic cadence that seemed designed to put you in a trance. After an initial line of address, the rest of the congregation responded with "Lord, hear our prayer."

"For all those suffering from pain and affliction."

"Lord, hear our prayer."

"For our most holy Father, Pope John Paul II."

"Lord, hear our prayer."

Sometimes the prayers would veer in the direction of the absurdly local, such as "For Victor, the usher at the eleven a.m. mass who suffered a broken foot last week."

"Lord, hear our prayer."

Other times the prayers expanded into what I considered the mindless pap of Disney movies and fairy tales.

"For global peace and international harmony among our world leaders."

"Lord, hear our prayer."

I suspected they could offer prayers for cottage cheese, Bulgarian shoe makers, or flotsam and jetsam in the Mississippi River and my father would still belt out, "Lord, hear our prayer" with such a volume that suggested enthusiasm alone granted a man access to the kingdom of heaven.

My father seemed to take special delight in Gospel readings. He stood before everyone else in church, drawing in a deep breath of anticipation, especially if they were from the Gospel of John, as though he had a vested interest in his namesake's writings the way he did in a Dolphins running play he had designed. "A new commandment I give unto you," the priest read from the pulpit. My father looked at me with a knowing nod: Listen up. *This one's for you.* "That ye love one another as I have loved you, that ye also love one another." Another stern nod from my father. I could read his thoughts: *Love, damn it.* A nod back from me: Got it. *Love, love, love.* Happy, happy, happy.

During communion, transubstantiation usually put my father in a prayer trance. I spent most of the time faking piety and scanning the communion line to look for attractive women. It seemed like a better use of time than asking my father whether he really believed that was the body of Christ. My mother and I had debated that one for years, each of us taking different sides at different times. Not my father. If the priest had proclaimed my father's individual communion wafer the left wrist of Christ, my father would have fully embraced it, never questioned it, and anticipated going back the following Sunday to complete the set with the right wrist of Christ.

Mass always ended with a song, my father's favorite, a chance to prove his faith once again with volume. Like the Responsorial Psalms, he would sing along to any lyrics that presented themselves in the hymnal. But if mass ended with one of his favorites, like the "Battle Hymn of the Republic," a song replete with swords, trampling, serpents crushed, lightning, righteousness, death, more death, and God marching on, then I found myself hoping none of the attractive women I had seen in the communion line sat anywhere near us. *Hi, nice to meet you. Yes, I'm the twenty-four-year-old whose father sang so loudly, portions of the ceiling collapsed. Perhaps we can have dinner together one night?*

The first few months following my mother's death my father and I took flowers to the cemetery after mass. Short, silent stretches of staring at the bronze grave markers reminded me why I still tried to go to church with my father, despite the ever-widening gap between our experiences and beliefs. I went in case he needed me. Without the scripted words of Catholicism, he grew fidgety, shifting his weight from side to side, beginning but never ending a sentence. "When do . . . I wonder . . ." He glanced around the cemetery looking for a familiar face standing at the foot of another gravesite, and when he found one he would give me a brief description, a tightly worded backstory similar to the cadence of a football scouting report: "Charlie and Claire Mastarego. Good people. Lost their son, Michael. Car accident. Twenty-five years old. Hit and run." Then more silence. More awkward weight shifting. We stood at the graves until we each sensed nothing dramatic was going to happen. No flash of light. No miracle. No brilliant insight. Just the chronic sense of loss that plumbs a depth words don't express and time can't contain.

Gradually our silences grew deeper and our visits to the cemetery grew shorter, until my father found a new way to spend time after mass on Sunday mornings.

Chapter Eight

WORST CHOICE FOR A BEST MAN

Over the next few months nine o'clock mass on Sunday morning extended into a morning of socializing for my father. He discovered that parishioners gathered on a covered deck just outside the church after services, nothing formal, just coffee and donuts, and my dad folded it into his Sunday morning routine. I joined him for the first one he attended. He had never hesitated to dive into a social gathering, but he seemed twitchy, his eyes darting about, his gait slowing as we approached the church deck. "We don't have to stay long. Just thought maybe we'd check it out," he said, as much to himself as to me.

The gathering revolved around watered-down coffee and donuts, whose chocolate icing my father seemed to enjoy slowly licking off his fingers, commenting too often how good they tasted: "Really good. Don't you think so?" He didn't approach anyone on the deck, and our conversation didn't veer far from the donuts. A man around my father's age walked up to us. He had slicked-back gray hair and weathered skin that reminded me of beef jerky. My dad introduced me to him, and after the man left a few minutes later my father gave me a scouting report on his problems, jogging my memory that I had first seen him at the cemetery.

"Charlie's son died in a car accident last year. Charlie hasn't been the same since. It just follows him everywhere."

I wondered whether it crossed my father's mind that people saw him the same way too.

Later we met Donna. Her husband had died from diabetes. Another man had lost his job. By the time I had finished a cup of coffee and two donuts, I had also met a man with cancer, a woman with glaucoma, and a priest everyone suspected of having a drinking problem. I went to work that day feeling the weight of depression covering me like an itchy, heavy burlap sack, the weight of the woes of the faithful at St. Bernadette's Catholic Church. I vowed to avoid future gatherings on the church deck. My dad became a regular.

In May, as we left church, my father asked me to stop by the church deck on my way to work and bring him his wallet that he had left at home. I arrived to find my father serving coffee, donuts, and smiles to a group of women. He was singing an Irish song, "Toora Loora," as he carried a tray of donuts to their table. He sang in a soft voice, not the booming baritone that could command a room's attention the way I had seen him do a hundred times before, but now in a gentle tone, barely above a whisper.

One of the women at the table stood and walked back with my father to the other end of the deck and helped him clean up the coffee station. He was whistling, "When Irish Eyes Are Smiling," and the woman, tall and fit with a warm smile, whistled along with him.

"Hey Bing Crosby, I brought your wallet," I said, walking up behind him.

"Thank you, Germ," he said. I hadn't heard him call me that nickname since I was a second grader. A science class introduction to germs spooked me, leaving me weary of every surface, glass, and eating utensil in our home and saddled me with an unfortunate nickname.

"Ladies, this is my son Gerry. The baby. Last of five. He's the sportscaster I was telling you about," my father said, beaming but without completing the loop by sharing their names with me.

I nodded and smiled at the table of unfamiliar faces. The woman I heard whistling with my father looked about his age, sixty. One of the other women at the table had a hungry look in her eyes that settled on my father for a second too long when she glanced his way. The third woman, a blonde with long, acrylic fingernails and a forced smile, was considerably younger, I presumed the daughter of one of the other women. Before I could ask their names, my father recruited me to help move a couple of coffee urns to a storage room in the back of the church.

Walking to the storage room, I saw my father limping. He had hip replacement surgery the year before my mother died. The doctors had told him he would eventually need the other one replaced as well, collateral damage from a life of playing and coaching football. Mom had taken care of him during the six-week recovery that followed surgery and complications. He had postponed his second hip replacement after she became ill.

As he hoisted one of the urns to a shelf, I noticed for the first time since my mom had died that my father no longer wore a wedding ring.

At the start of summer Dan Sekanovich moved into his own house, and on nights I didn't work, I saw less and less of my father. "Church functions," he usually said when I asked him where he was the night before, trying not to sound like a parent interrogating a teenager. By mid-June I began to wonder whether priests attended fewer church functions than my father.

Phone calls to my brothers and sister only agitated my suspicion that my father had an interest in someone that went beyond coffee and donuts. I seemed to keep running into the tall woman with gray hair and a warm smile whom I had met on the church deck. She made a point of saying hello to me after church. Once, she stopped me in the grocery store on one of my trips for dog food and spaghetti sauce to comment on a story I had done on the University of Miami baseball team. When she noticed what I had in my shopping basket she added, "I never thought about mixing spaghetti sauce with dog food. Let me know how that turns out." We both laughed. I noticed she had let a much older woman who only had a few items in her shopping cart go in front of her at the checkout line. When her turn came she went out of her way to talk to the cashier and bag boys. *Could this be Dad's girlfriend?* I wondered.

Each week more and more of my spaghetti went uneaten. Jim and Ruth Ann called more often. They wanted to know: Was Dad seeing someone? What was her name? I didn't know, and I didn't know how to ask him. "I think you'll like the woman who I think he's seeing," I had told Ruth Ann. "She's tall, elegant. Has gray hair. Attractive." I could hear the grin in Ruth Ann's voice, feel the shake of her head, a gentle admonishment for my having only a vague idea of Dad's foray into a social life. "The woman you think he's seeing," Ruth Ann said, "have you asked him?" I had never been able to talk to my father about girls *I* had an interest in—how would I bring up the topic of someone *he* was attracted to? I did what I had seen my father do during emotionally stressful times: I worked more and ignored more. Until I couldn't.

Dad invited me to dinner to meet a friend of his.

We went to an Italian restaurant in a strip mall a couple of miles from our house, a fancier place than either of us considered when we exhausted the spaghetti pot in our kitchen. This place had white tablecloths, a wine rack on the back wall, Pavarotti playing on speakers hidden by trellises covered with plastic vines.

Before I left the house I had called Ruth Ann, who still lived in New Jersey with her husband and young daughter. "Any chance you want to fly down and meet me in case I need backup support?

"How far along can this be? This is Dad we're talking about," she said.

"What should I call Dad's 'friend'?"

"Start with finding out her name this time."

My father had arrived before me. I saw him sitting at a table near the back of the restaurant. His friend had arrived too, and not the one I expected. She wasn't the gray-haired woman from church and the grocery store, the one with a welcoming smile. She was the bleached blonde I had seen on the church deck, the one with a smile as contrived as her acrylic nails, a woman who looked not much older than my sister. A college-aged girl sat next to her.

My father stood as I approached the table, a formality that was out of character.

"Gerry, this is Shirley," he said, making a sweeping gesture toward her with his left hand as I reached the table. He had a broad and beaming smile. "And this is her daughter Gina," he said, nodding toward the sandy-haired college girl across the table.

During the course of the meal I watched my father occasionally reach out his left hand and wrap it around Shirley's hand. Each time I saw him do it, I felt a lump in my throat like a bite of lasagna was wedged in my esophagus. For most of the evening I felt like I was having an out-of-body experience, the kind you read about people having after a nearly fatal car accident. I watched myself absorbing wave after wave of shock as my father poured red wine and details about Shirley's life with an equally heavy hand.

Gina was the oldest of three kids. Shirley was an elementary school teacher. My father lamented what a deadbeat her ex-husband had been, how hard it was for Shirley to make ends meet. He knew all about her problems and didn't seem to recognize how many of them revolved around money.

Shirley leaned toward me as dessert arrived. She blinked twice, her eyelashes swollen with mascara. She made a theatrical gesture of reaching for my father's hand, interlocking her fingers in his, slowly lifting their intertwined hands off the table like a fisherman hoisting a marlin for a photo on the dock as she said, "So tell me more about you."

I could feel my mouth moving, words were coming out, but inside I was scrambling, trying to figure out a way to undo this night, this meeting, this woman. I settled for telling her I worked a lot like my father, all the while thinking, *I'll tell you about me. I'm a guy who watched his father bury his mother six months ago and is now watching him fall into the oldest trap in the world, a younger woman with a big chest and bigger needs. I'm a guy who's wondering, Christ Almighty what is my father doing? I'm a guy wondering how he's going to call his sister tomorrow and say, "Houston, we have a problem."*

My problems were only beginning.

By the end of June our house had fallen into full neglect. The pool water, now a murky aqua, had a green algae line forming on the edges of the surface. My expanding workload at the TV station left me little time to do much more than sleep at home. One or two times a week I stopped at a Burdines department store on my way to work to buy a dress shirt when I didn't have time to do laundry. The washing machine remained a mystery to my father. And the next-door neighbors had begun to complain about our dog.

Dixie had been my mom's companion. Now, as life and traffic had leaked out of our house, she spent hours aggravating neighbors with a high-pitched wail, a plea for company. Work had become my companion, and judging from the height of the grass in our front yard, my father spent less time at home than I did.

He called me at work one evening, something he only did when we had no spaghetti, dog food, or leftovers to feed Dixie. "I think we're going to have to do something about the dog," he said.

By "we," he meant me.

"The neighbors have been over for a third time to complain about her howling. She tore up one of the couch cushions today." He paused, awkwardly searching for the words to complete his indictment. Then he blurted them out: "Shirley came by the other day. She commented on the smell."

Shirley. She monopolized his time and attention. She occasionally sent over food—sausage and peppers, ziti, casseroles—and when she did my dad made a point of letting me know, commenting on her generosity. I fed Shirley's food to Dixie. My father wanted me to give away Dixie, find a better home for her, a place with kids, a bigger backyard, a family who could devote some time and attention to her. He didn't realize families like that bought new puppies, pure breeds—cocker spaniels, chocolate labs—from pet stores. They didn't want a four-year-old mutt with spotted fur and the pedigree of a gypsy.

A friend of mine named Lee Ann, who had dated a mutual friend and, over the previous few years, become a better friend of mine, helped me locate a shelter with a high success rate of finding new homes for animals. I drove Dixie to the animal shelter in downtown Hollywood, stopping along the way to play in a park, watching Dixie sprint after the tennis ball I threw, aching every time she darted back to me, the ball in her mouth, tail wagging, expressing a loyalty I couldn't return. A stray my mother had saved, what chance did this dog have of finding a second savior? As I began to hand her across the counter at the shelter, tears streaming down my face, Dixie looked back at me, her eyes wide in confusion, heartbreak, an accusation of betrayal. The young woman I handed Dixie to said an older woman had come by the shelter earlier that day, looking for a dog just like Dixie for companionship. She promised me Dixie would have a new home by tomorrow. I made her promise me again before I released my hands from Dixie, my fingertips running across her soft coat a last time, leaving me feeling like I had surrendered the last touchstone left from my mom.

Lee Ann called me later in the day to ask how things went with Dixie. I stumbled to explain how deeply shards of guilt and betrayal had embedded in my heart. Lee Ann invited me over for dinner, and as much as I wanted to eat something other than spaghetti, I asked if we could do it on another night when I could be better company.

Walking through the living room the next day, a glint from the top of the organ that had sat idle since my mother died caught my eye. My mother's bracelet from the Baltimore Colts Super Bowl V win, an exact replica of the top of my father's ring, reflecting the sunlight, had grabbed my attention. I hadn't seen it in years. I put it in my desk drawer for safekeeping. The next day when I got home from work I ran into my father, whom I hadn't seen for days. He was wearing dress slacks and a new shirt, and for the first time in my life he smelled like expensive cologne.

"Have you seen Mom's bracelet?" he asked.

"Yeah, did you leave it out?"

"I got it out to give to Shirley. I was telling her about it and thought it might make a nice gift, but I couldn't remember where I put it."

For the first time in my life I understood how my father had felt every time I saw him with his jaw clenched, his eyebrows pulled low like a sweatshirt hood over his dark, angry eyes. A volcanic rush of emotions clotted at the base of my throat then exploded from my mouth: "Goddamn it, Dad! That's Mom's! This house is Mom's! That ring is our history! It's not a bauble to give to . . . to . . . your damn girlfriend!" The last word seemed to spit itself out, a word too blunt, too honest, too real.

"But I sort of promised it to Shirley already," he said meekly. My father saying something meekly only made me madder.

"I just gave away Mom's dog. You aren't giving her bracelet away." My voice quivered on the border of panic and anger. My father took a half step backward, his face slack, his mouth open. I walked out of the room, waiting for him to explode. I only heard the rusty creak and the click of the front door closing behind him.

Shirley began showing up around the house more often, usually on Saturdays when Dad had free time. She wore her dirty blond hair up, accentuating her round face. She usually arrived wearing make-up—blue eye shadow—and a tight-fitting top.

The more I saw of Shirley, the less I liked the idea of my father seeing her. She was an interloper in our house, turning a disapproving eye toward the kitchen. She would wonder out loud why we kept that garage the way we did, with Mom's old bolts of fabric still laid out on an old ping-pong table.

A housekeeper, who Shirley recommended, appeared. Mold and disorder faded, but so did the fingerprints of Mom's touches around the house. More and more memories of Mom evaporated. Her sewing machine disappeared. Her organ went to the church. Her side of the closet my parents had shared was now empty. A picture of Shirley and Dad smiling together at a church social showed up in a picture frame in the living room.

By the start of the 1986 Dolphins season my father's deteriorating hip reduced his stride to a waddle. He never mentioned his obvious pain, but a grimace and furrowed brow accompanying each step on and off the practice field made it obvious he needed another hip replacement.

My career continued to take shape. I now traveled with the Dolphins covering their road games as well as home games for my TV station. The first game of the season took my dad and me to San Diego, where we began a new tradition: sitting on the team bench before pregame warm-ups began. Sitting gave him a break from the pain of standing on a failing hip. It also gave us a chance to catch up. With nothing linking us to home but the need to sleep, a week or two could pass without our paths crossing anywhere but the parking lot of the Dolphins' training facility.

Since the bracelet incident my father seemed to tiptoe around me the way I had done for years with him, avoiding talking about Shirley, sticking to safer topics.

"Some place, San Diego," my father said. The smell of freshly cut grass rose from the cool shadow that had swallowed the Dolphins bench on the sideline near the middle of the field.

"The view doesn't really change from down here, does it?" I said, staring across the perfectly manicured field as players began to walk out of the locker room.

"Just the weather and the logo in the middle."

A football field is a geometric universe. A rectangle, 120 yards long, 53 yards wide. All lines on the field meet at a right angle. A thick, white stripe, six feet wide, runs around the perimeter of the field. Inside the field straight white lines run from one sideline to the next, five yards apart. Large white numbers straddling every other line count the yards from the goal line—10, 20, 30, 40—to midfield and then count back down again—40, 30, 20, 10—to the other end zone.

In the center of the field the fifty-yard line bisected the Chargers thunderbolt logo.

"What are you going to do about that hip, Dad?"

"I'll deal with it after the season. Can't do much with it."

I could see the uncertainty on his face. Could he hold out that long? Would he get his mobility back? Could he keep coaching? All unanswerable questions that contrasted with the perfectly balanced world that sat before us, a world of order and measure. First and ten. Second and five. Third and two. A world with a neatly painted border that divided every action into one of two categories: in bounds and out of bounds. No shades of gray.

But a gray shadow of worry had followed my father to the bench.

"I suppose the hip limits your social life too with Shirley?" I asked, trying to feel my way around the topic.

He stared across the field. "Limits everything."

"Whoa."

"Not that, smartass. She's a good Catholic woman." Now he looked directly at me, his eyes a period. Full stop.

"You guys see a lot of each other these days, huh?" I found myself marooned in an awkward place. I sensed Dad wanted to talk about Shirley, explore feelings he hadn't encountered since he dated Mom in the window of years that followed World War II. But I didn't like Shirley. I had a bad feeling about her, or was it just my awkwardness with seeing my Dad hold hands with a woman and then melt into a pie-eyed stare of happiness that belonged to a teenager?

"I suppose," he said, turning his attention back to the field, his big hands resting against the metal bench, tapping out the beat of a song pounding through the stadium's speakers, a strong, soulful woman's voice wrapping around the words "saving all my love for you."

"She's good. Who is this?" my father asked.

"Whitney Houston."

"You really like her, don't you?" I asked.

"I guess. First time I've heard her."

"Not her. Shirley.

"Oh. Uh, yeah, I suppose."

"How old is she?" I asked.

"Whitney Houston?"

"No. Shirley."

He hesitated, then focused his attention to San Diego Chargers head coach Don Coryell, who was walking in our direction. "Don, how are you?" my father said, his voice a little too loud and dressed in a tone of relief. He introduced me to Coryell, a man with the thin build of a distance runner and bushy eyebrows that arched above his dark eyes that looked like two black holes punched into the entrance to a coal shaft. I looked on as my father and Coryell commiserated about job pressures, rookies, and the grind of their schedules.

"Sorry to hear about your wife," Coryell said. My father nodded and blurted out something that sounded like "tough, real tough." I noticed he didn't say anything about missing Mom. When Coryell walked away my father tilted his weight to his right and pushed himself up from the bench, gritting his teeth. "I better get to work," he said. I wished him good luck and watched him waddle in the direction of the far end zone, slowly crossing the thirty-yard line, twenty, ten, with the weight of Coryell's condolences and my questions about Shirley leaving him as off balance as his balky hip.

The Chargers destroyed the Dolphins, beating them 50–28.

After the game I made my way, along with the rest of the media, beneath the stadium to a dank tunnel with the musty smell of wet dirt, where Don Shula held his postgame press conference. Shula arrived with his hair as tousled as his ire.

I had worked my way to the front of the media pack, standing directly in front of Shula, who held a large paper cup filled with Coke. He delivered a short recap of his impressions from the beating and snapped, "Questions?" More of a command than an invitation.

As Shula raised his cup to take a drink, I began to ask my first question, hoping speed and aggressiveness would catch his eye and ear before a more senior reporter monopolized his attention. No sooner had a handful of words left my mouth, "Coach, did the quick—" than someone bumped my elbow from behind. My microphone plunged into the bottom of Shula's cup, dumping his Coke across his chest.

He glowered at me, the heat of a flamethrower melting me into silence as I tried to creep backward into the pack of reporters.

On the flight home my father sought me out in the back of the plane. "Heard you caught the boss's attention," he said with a grin that let me know he had seen that same look from Don Shula on plenty of occasions.

"Shula say anything?" I asked.

"Just that you didn't finish your question."

"Uh, kind of chickened out today," I admitted.

"Yeah, me too," he said. "Shirley's forty."

For a second time in the same day I couldn't think of anything to say as I watched my father waddle back to the front of the plane.

Three weeks later we sat on the Meadowlands bench in East Rutherford, New Jersey, and our conversation turned to Shirley's three kids: two girls and a boy, one in college, two in high school.

"They haven't had much of a father figure," he said. I translated that into his desire to be a family again. He needed a family again. Time and tragedy had whittled ours down to him and me, and I was rarely home. My brothers lived in Baltimore, my sister in New Jersey. They had their own families, and an occasional weekend visit didn't fill the loneliness.

At the beginning of October, in Foxboro, Massachusetts, home of the New England Patriots, my father sounded like a man at a crossroads. Worry and pain creased his forehead. On the verge of a three-game losing streak, the Dolphins looked as awkward on the field as my father did walking the sidelines. His voice had a darkness to it, mirroring the early chill of fall. "If we don't play better soon, my future might involve something other than football," he said. The cloudiness of the New England fall mirrored the uncertainty that had crept into his gaze. He would turn sixty-one in December, unofficially old for an NFL coach.

His was a carefully measured world. Once the game began, every second that came off the game clock moved him in the direction of the numbers that defined his life and separated success from failure: the final score. The Patriots handed the Dolphins a third straight loss, 34–7.

In Indianapolis, where the Colts had moved three years before, we sat in the controlled climate of an indoor stadium, looking at the familiar blue-and-white Colts uniforms as players trickled onto the field for pregame warm-ups beneath the white roof of the Hoosier Dome.

"Those uniforms still look great," my father said, nodding toward Colts running back Randy McMillan, who stood across the field in his blue Colts jersey with white shoulder stripes, white pants with two blue stripes running down the sides. "But they seem out of place."

The synthetic field lacked the loamy smell of dirt and grass. The Colts we knew, the ones we still on occasion thought of as home, had smudges of dirt on their jerseys and pants, a cold wind blowing across their field, and Baltimore in front of their name. The Colts in Indianapolis, in a dome, looked too pristine, borrowed, and trying too hard, the same way my father looked with Shirley.

"Ever want to be a head coach again?" I asked, trying to read his thoughts.

"Doesn't matter what I want. They don't give guys my age another chance. I'd settle for a new hip and my same old job."

I had never before heard him use the word *settle*.

November brought a trip to Cleveland and the stadium my father had played in during his career with the Browns in the fifties. The chilly autumn air off Lake Erie swirled around the cavernous, horseshoe-shaped Municipal Stadium.

"Did you enjoy living here?" I asked.

"We did. Crappy weather but good people. Mom loved the people here." It was the first time he had mentioned Mom in months. "I wasn't much older than you are now when we got married." He looked up toward the light stanchions perched on top of the stadium and grew quiet as memories flooded down on him and the cold dampness rose from the grass field. "She used to sit over there," he pointed toward the closed end of the horseshoe, near the Browns' entrance to the field. "I used to stop on my way to the locker room to look for her after games. It was our routine." He was looking now at empty seats, and I wondered whether he saw the outline of the memory of my mom as a twenty-five-year-old, waiting for him after a Browns win, her smile and eyes sparkling, their life together still in front of them, two young adults—naïve, hopeful, and unaware of the heartbreak that would eventually divide them the way lightning cleaves an old tree.

"Good times," he whispered. "Good times." His voice faded away, and we sat in silence until the start of pregame warm-ups pried him from the bench and sent me to the press box.

A week later, in Buffalo, winter greeted us with five-foot-tall mounds of snow plowed into the corners of the field at Rich Stadium. The night before, my father had asked me to join him for dinner with some of Shirley's cousins—Buffalo was her hometown. I went as his wingman, an easy out if things went poorly: *Sorry we have to go so soon, my son has production meetings back at the hotel*—meetings I didn't have and, in the end, an excuse he didn't need.

Shirley's relatives, old friends, and neighbors converged like streams, one indistinguishable from the next, but all friendly and welcoming. Total strangers opened their home, fed us, and treated us like visiting dignitaries. My father had seemed at ease—laughing, drinking, and eating with people he had never met before. He held court at the dinner table, sharing football stories, dropping names from Dan Marino to Johnny Unitas to Bills quarterback Jim Kelly: "Helluva quarterback that Kelly. Too bad we have to beat him tomorrow." More stories. More rigatoni. More beers.

In the hours leading up to the game we sat on the Dolphins bench, bundled in parkas, the field in front of us a green slab of frozen Astroturf, the geometry unchanged. Two of the Dolphins' defensive linemen, Bob Baumhower and Doug Betters, milled in front of us, walking the field the way tourists walk a Civil War battlefield, visualizing action, imagining the battle, digesting it.

"Seemed like a nice family," my father said.

I couldn't disagree.

He had taken Shirley's family for a test drive of sorts and found them a perfect fit. Blue collar, football fans, beer drinkers, genuinely nice people. I found it odd that none of Shirley's relatives talked about her much or whether she left Buffalo for a guy, a job, or just to get away from the weather.

Dan Marino walked by the bench, nodding at my father and me. We exchanged a syllable or two, the currency of communication in the hours leading up to a football game. Marino looked up at the low, gray sky with the attention of a broker watching the direction of a stock market move. I looked at my father with the same anxious curiosity.

"I could get used to being around a nice family like that," my father said unprompted. It was his way of indirectly talking about Shirley.

By December the Dolphins had a 6–7 record. The playoffs looked unlikely. My father tilted side to side now when he walked and sucked a stream of air between his gritted teeth when he moved. Dark bags had settled under his eyes. His painful walk from the locker room brought him to the team bench in the Super Dome in New Orleans, a mammoth indoor stadium with cushioned seats in the stands and precise lighting that illuminated the field like a Broadway stage. Every step my father had taken to reach the bench hurt to watch. We sat silently for several minutes, giving my dad a chance to catch his breath. "Hard place to win, with so many distractions," he said, as two attractive women walked by us. "Pleasant distractions at least."

He read my silence perfectly. "Doesn't hurt to look at the menu," he said, adding a grin and a wink.

"Want me to get their numbers?" I asked. "Set up a double date?"

"I doubt Shirley would appreciate that," he said.

I let the conversation fade back to silence.

The last road trip of the season took us to Anaheim, where the Dolphins played the Rams. I found my father already sitting on the bench,

enjoying the Southern California sunshine, staring down at his size fourteen, triple-wide shoes that snugly held his bearlike feet, the only thing
that kept him from toppling over when he tried to walk.

"How's the bank account growing?" he asked.

"Surprisingly fast." Most of my check went to savings. My dad didn't
want me to share expenses. He wanted me to save money.

"Enjoy it while you can. You'll have your own family one day, with
more bills than you'll know what to do with," he said, adding an impish
grin. "Kinda like me for the last thirty-five years."

"Feel good to finally bank some money of your own?"

"Kind of like you," he said. "Doing it while I can."

Eric Dickerson, the Rams Pro Bowl running back, jogged past us,
pulling my father's attention with him. "Guy's a beast," my father said with
a tone of admiration. "I hope he doesn't run over us today. We need this
win."

A break-even record would lead to fewer changes in the off-season
than a losing record. In football change begins with the old and the
unhealthy. My father showed signs of both. His only escape from pain
and uncertainty came in the span of time between kickoff and when the
game clock read :00, a three-hour respite in a cocoon of straight lines and
straightforward outcomes.

In Anaheim the day ended with the Dolphins beating the Rams 37–31.

The Dolphins' playoff chances came down to the final game of the
season against New England in the Orange Bowl. I had arrived home late
the night before from a work trip. The warmth of South Florida in late
December brought a welcome change of temperature from the previous
three days I had spent in Pennsylvania shooting preview stories for the
University of Miami's upcoming National Championship game against
Penn State.

"You'll never guess who I did a story with," I said, after my father had
settled onto the metal bench ten yards away from the sideline at midfield
at the Orange Bowl.

"Fill me in."

Mike Kozlowski jogged by the bench, pointed to me, and said with a laugh, "You ready to go if we need you?" I felt a tickle of pride that Kozlowski remembered the hour we had spent together on the practice field a few summers before.

"God help us if we do," my father said as he smacked me on the leg and added a laugh.

"I did a feature story on Penn State's defensive coordinator. A guy named Jerry Sandusky. Kind of ironic, huh?"

"How did the story turn out?"

Just then Dan Sekanovich walked up to us. "What's happening, Roomies? How's the dorm without me?"

"Hey Dan," my dad said. "Ever coach with a guy named Jerry Sandusky?"

"No, but I lived with a guy with that name not that long ago," he said, adding his basset hound smile.

"Pretty much how the story turned out," I said. "Part coincidence, part confusion. He joked that I might have to start calling myself 'Gerry with a G' if Penn State wins so Miami fans don't blame me for the Hurricanes' loss."

In the final minutes of the Dolphins game I walked from the press box down to the field to shoot stand-ups for my story for that night's eleven o'clock news. I stood on the sidelines near the goal line closest to the Dolphins' locker room as the final seconds came off the game clock and the final score ended the Dolphins' playoff hopes. New England 34, Miami 27.

I waited for my father to walk by. He hobbled badly, groaning as he exhaled through his tightly clamped teeth with every step he took toward the locker room. Everyone could see his physical pain, but I knew he felt the sharp edges of worry and doubt grinding against each other too. Each awkward step took him away from the simplicity of measuring life in sixty-minute strips of time on a field precisely marked with straight white lines beneath a scoreboard that illuminated success or failure. He didn't know whether he would ever get to walk back into this world.

It was the end of a season that looked ordinary in the standings. Eight wins, eight losses. But it was also the end of an extraordinary season—our season, the one we had gone through together, one conversation at a time, one painful walk at a time, one bench at a time. As I watched my father disappear into the locker room, I suspected our time of trying to figure out the future together would disappear soon too.

Christmas lured Jim, Ruth Ann, and their families to South Florida under the guise of a holiday get-together. Tired of my conflicting reports, they wanted to meet Shirley. Whispers peppered with concern from my brother Jim, sister Ruth, and her husband, Bob, dotted our late-night conversations at the kitchen table. *Keep him from making a huge mistake. Mom's only been gone for a year. Shirley's too young. Does Dad know how much college tuition costs now? Christ, she has three kids. What if surgery doesn't work on his hip? How long will Shirley hang around then?*

The night Jim and Ruth Ann met Shirley at the house for the first time I was at work, so the three of us went to a local bar, Uncle Al's, to talk when I got home. A layer of cigarette smoke hovered above our pool table. Jim ordered a pitcher of Budweiser, and the three of us played pool, talking over the backdrop of country music. We ignored the advice of the Hank Williams Jr. song "Mind Your Own Business."

"You know her hair isn't really blonde," Jim said, lining up a shot. He dropped the two ball in the far corner. "And that smile, Jesus, could it have been more insincere?"

"In fairness, can you imagine how nervous the poor woman was meeting us?" Ruth Ann said.

Jim missed his next shot.

I dropped the eleven ball in the corner pocket but missed badly on my next shot, barely scraping the twelve ball with the cue ball.

While Jim lined up an easy shot I asked, "Did she bring food?"

"Yeah, what's with her cooking? Who calls pasta macaroni?" He dropped the four ball in a corner pocket and turned his attention to the seven ball on the far side of the table. "Was that a diamond in the Dolphins pendant Dad bought her?"

"Umm hmm," I said.

"He does seem happy," Ruth Ann said.

Jim missed his shot. "Shit. He acts like a teenager around her."

I tapped in an easy shot Jim left me, putting the twelve ball in the side pocket. "He does seem happy. And he does act like a teenager. And she does seem phony. You're both right. That's the problem," I said, as my attempt to bang the thirteen ball at a forty-five-degree angle into the corner pocket instead sent the cue ball to the far side of the table and back without touching another ball.

"You guys suck at pool," Ruth Ann said, grabbing the pool stick from my hand.

"Not as bad as Dad sucks at picking a girlfriend," Jim said.

"And I wouldn't mind if it was just that, a girlfriend," I added, watching Ruth Ann drop the thirteen ball, then the fourteen.

"Speaking of girlfriends, you seem to be seeing a lot of Lee Ann lately," Jim said as he punched me playfully in the shoulder. "Still just friends?"

Ruth Ann banked the cue ball off the side cushion, moving it around a cluster of solid balls, and sent the nine ball with a solid click into a corner pocket. "What's Lee Ann think of Shirley?" Ruth Ann asked.

"She thinks if Dad is so smitten, we better find a way to get along with her."

"How much are we playing for?" Ruth asked as she buried the ten ball in a side pocket.

"I think a hundred bucks is fair," I said as Ruth Ann put away the fifteen ball and turned her attention to the eight ball in the middle of the table.

"Thanks for spending my money," Jim said as he reached out his right arm and put me in a headlock. "You know, I'll bet Dad has already spent more money on Shirley then he ever spent on Mom."

"He's going to spend a lot more than he ever imagined if he stays on this path," Ruth Ann said. Her shot sounded like a pistol firing, as the cue ball cracked into the eight ball and sent it into the corner pocket, far side, exactly where she had called it.

She stood up, right hand on her hip as she held out her left hand to Jimmy. "Pay up, brother," she said with a grin that lifted her glasses. "Or you can just buy the next pitcher of beer."

A few nights after Christmas I found my father sitting by the pool. Shirley's influence continued to surface. A maintenance company now kept the pool water gleaming. The place no longer resembled a frat house.

Jim didn't like Shirley. Jack, my oldest brother, took a neutral position. My sister remained the target of my father's hopes.

"I want your sister to really like Shirley," my father said. Ruth Ann's approval would tip the balance of opinion. In his eyes Ruth held more than just Mom's name; she held her proxy.

I had grabbed a plate of leftover lasagna, even if Shirley had made it, and pulled up a chair. "Have a direct conversation with Ruth," I said. "Address all the concerns—age, health, loneliness, wanting a family life again—something a little more consistent than sitting on a bench with me in stadiums all around the country. And remind Ruth that you didn't pick her spouse, but you did accept him."

The more I said, the more he smiled. He could see I understood. He couldn't, however, see that I didn't like him spending all of his time with the only woman he had dated since Mom died. He couldn't see how torn I felt. I understood my brother and sister's concerns, but I also understood my father's fear that a pretty, younger woman might never show him so much interest again. I had waffled over the past months in my support. I don't know whether he could see how much it hurt me to see him falling helplessly in love with a woman who wasn't my mother. But he could see I had finished off my plate of lasagna.

"Pretty good cook, isn't she?"

"Not as good as say . . . my spaghetti . . . but not bad." We both laughed.

"I'm having surgery next week," he said as he pushed himself out of his chair and began to hobble toward his bedroom. He stopped and added, "I might need a little extra help when I get home from the hospital," he said. "The kind of help I'm not comfortable asking for from Shirley."

The surgery went well, and during the week he spent in the hospital, every time I visited my father Shirley sat next to his bed, bragging about his progress, talking about how good he would feel walking without a painful limp.

"He can keep coaching," she said to me during one of my visits while my father slept. "Coach Shula called him today, said he wanted him back next season. Your father won't feel like damaged goods anymore. He'll be young again." I wondered whether Shirley knew that no one had considered my dad young since he fired heavy mortar at German soldiers who occupied France during World War II—not his brothers, not his sisters, not his wife, certainly not his children.

When my father returned home I learned about the extra help he needed. Doctors cautioned my father not to get in or out of the shower by himself so as to avoid slipping and damaging his new hip. The same held for going to the bathroom. He needed me to wipe his rear end, as twisting to do it himself could damage the hip until it set firmly in place.

Each trip to the shower or the toilet put my father in my hands, literally. The first time—and every time after—he gave me a look unlike any I had seen since the day I handed Dixie across the counter at the animal shelter: an unspoken fear, a dread that this might not work. Without saying a word, I wrapped my arms around his chest from behind and guided him across the tile floor of his bathroom. I prayed he stayed upright, straining to keep my arms secure and around his barrel chest, knowing a fall could mean the end of his career, the end of his hopes of moving forward with his life.

Three weeks into his recovery, when doctors cleared him to manage for himself, he walked toward the bathroom, and out of habit I rose from our sofa to follow him. "I've got this now," he said, holding up his left hand, a stop sign for me. He paused in the doorway and our eyes locked. "But I wouldn't have gotten here without you."

Once he had fully healed and began driving again, my father asked me to meet him for dinner to celebrate. Shirley joined us at the same restaurant where I had first met her months before. It was my father's way of expressing all the gratitude he had for helping him. He was never good with words, and I certainly didn't expect the words he was about to express. After dinner, as we finished a plate of cannolis for dessert, my father reached out his left hand to hold Shirley's hand. Then he turned to me and said, "Gerry, I've asked Shirley to marry me, and I'd like you to be my best man."

I just about choked on my after-dinner mint. It's not that I was surprised my dad had asked Shirley to marry him; it was the last part that left me tangled. The best man? I knew I wasn't. The ambivalent man, perhaps. Happy to see my father smiling again but worried about the speed he accelerated into a new life, a new relationship. We had buried Mom little more than year ago. I still missed her. Am I disloyal to my mother if I stand for my father at a wedding to a woman whose motives I still question? Am I being loyal to my father by standing at his side while he says, "I do," when I want him to say, "I'll wait"?

My silence lapsed into clumsy.

I had always presumed my father would attend my wedding one day, give his blessing to the woman I chose to marry, not the other way around. He had never asked me a question that made him smile more and me flinch more.

I finally heard the words that navigated their way out of my mouth: "Dad, that's great news. I would be honored to be your best man." I plastered on a smile and wished I could navigate my way out of standing so close to my father at a wedding that would change all of our lives.

— Chapter Nine —

BEGINNING OF THE END

My father's marriage took him to a new house in Hollywood, Florida, ten minutes from our old one, and a new family with Shirley and her three kids. I bought a townhouse in the adjacent town, Pembroke Pines, and we both began new lives. His NFL coaching career lasted another eight seasons, all with the Miami Dolphins, only one of which I shared with him. At the end of the 1987 season I eloped with my fiancée, Lee Ann, while covering the Fiesta Bowl in Tempe, Arizona. Lee Ann had green eyes glittered with dazzling flecks of yellow and a compact mouth that expanded into a smile so big it left you wondering how a woman only five feet tall could fit so many perfectly straight teeth into her small mouth. The freckles on the bridge of her nose seemed to sprinkle onto her cheeks when she smiled, forming a warm canopy of red above her white smile, the kind of smile that made you feel better about most everything just by being in front of it.

I heard a mixture of relief and disappointment in my father's voice the night I called him from Arizona. The disappointment vanished when I let him know he was the first person I had called. The relief surfaced soon enough too: "So this means I don't have to buy a new suit, right?"

The following year a weeknight sportscaster's job at WBAL-TV took me and Lee Ann to Baltimore, where we started our own family, and for the rest of my father's life he and I had a long-distance relationship—phone calls, holiday visits, road trips to Philadelphia and Washington when the Dolphins' schedule took him to those nearby cities.

His last year on the sidelines, like so many in his career, carried Super Bowl hopes late into the season. This time I had to share in his joy from three thousand miles away.

The Dolphins had advanced to the AFC divisional playoff game against the San Diego Chargers, just two wins away from going to the Super Bowl.

For weeks newspaper articles in Miami had speculated my father's career might end with the season. He had just turned seventy, the mile marker of ancient in pro sports. The night before the game I called my dad at the team hotel in San Diego.

"One last shot at a Super Bowl. That's all I want," Dad said. "Might as well go out on top."

He hadn't talked directly with Don Shula about retirement. They had what my father called, "an understanding." In other words, like with so many issues that fell outside the precise, geometric white lines of a football field and the play selection of an important third down, he had talked around the issue. I could imagine how it had played out, like so many exchanges I had seen my father have, an artful dance between confrontation and avoidance: A brief exchange in a hallway outside the locker room. Shula with his reading glasses perched near the end of his nose, talking while he glanced over an injury report. My dad, caught off guard, trying to save a measure of dignity in a decision that he would want to look like he made.

"John, what are you thinking about next year?"

"I don't know. If I feel good, and I do. Probably wait and see."

"Not sure we have that luxury. To wait, I mean. I want to stay out ahead of this."

"Well, then, I, uh . . ."

"Alright."

And from that point forward my father knew he had reached the end. Or the end had reached him.

The next day I had the fireplace going in the family room in our house north of Baltimore when the San Diego Chargers kicked off to the Dolphins.

Katy, our precocious six-year-old, who had a mouth shaped like my mother's, an angel's wings, and a tongue as quick as a devil's trident, played with her baby brother, Zack, on a blanket Lee Ann had spread out in the middle of the floor.

The Dolphins took a commanding 21–6 lead by halftime.

I added a couple of logs to the fire as the second half began, and as I returned to the floor next to the kids, cold soda splashed against my forearm. Katy shrieked, "Zack knocked over my drink!"

"I'll get a new blanket. Watch the game," Lee Ann said to me, her small mouth expanding into a reassuring smile.

"Big third down for the Dolphins to set the tone for the second half," Dick Enberg, the play-by-play announcer on the NBC broadcast, said.

"Daddy, can I have a cookie?" Katy asked.

"Sure, sweetie," I said, not thinking for a second what I had agreed to, my eyes locked on the TV.

Zack's hysterical wail jolted my attention away from the game.

"I'm sorry," Katy said.

She had stepped on his hand.

"I didn't mean to, Daddy," Katy said before joining her brother in a burst of tears.

I picked up Zack to console him and pulled Katy next to me, trying to calm both of them down.

"Gerry, can you help me?" Lee Ann shouted from the stairs. "Quickly," she added.

"Shit," I mumbled as I put down my kids.

"Oh Daddy, that's a bad word," Katy said.

As I reached the hallway, out of the sightline of the TV, I heard Dick Enberg's voice rise in a tone of disbelief: "What are the chances of that?"

"Quickly, Gerry, the drinks are spilling." Lee Ann stood halfway down the stairs, a blanket falling off her left arm, a tray of drinks balanced in her right hand, Zack's pacifier dangling from her pinky finger.

"Grab the blanket before I trip on it."

I snatched the blanket and sprinted back to the family room.

"The safety," Enberg said, "makes the score 21–8."

"Shit, what happened?"

"Daddy's saying bad words, Mommy," Katy said to Lee Ann.

As the Chargers began their next drive, Lee Ann held Zack while feeding him dinner from a baby food jar of ham and peas.

The phone rang.

Lee Ann looked to me, crinkling her nose, holding up the spoon. "Can you get it? It might be my parents."

As I turned to reach for the phone, I heard Enberg's voice peak again.

When I wheeled back around Chargers players were jumping around, celebrating.

"The phone, honey."

"Hello," I barked.

"Hi, is Lee Ann San-doosky there?" A sugary voice asked, mispronouncing our last name.

"She's busy. Who is it?

"I'm calling because our company has replaced the windows on several of your neighbors' houses, and I'd like to talk to you about . . . "

I slammed down the phone.

"The extra point will make it 21–15," the announcer said.

"What happened?" I asked Lee Ann, who was now on her knees, scrubbing the rug.

"I don't know," she said. "Zack knocked the spoon out of my hand."

"Is Daddy going to say more bad words?" Katy asked.

"Only if someone interrupts me again," I said, hearing the echo of my father's voice.

In the fourth quarter the Dolphins clung to a six-point lead. The Chargers had the ball with less than a minute to play.

"Don't touch that, honey," Lee Ann yelled.

Katy's wail ripped my attention from the game. She had touched the grill covering the fireplace.

Lee Ann reached her before I could. "Get some ice in a hand towel," she said.

When I returned to the family room with a towel filled with ice, I heard Dick Enberg say, "Nineteen unanswered points for San Diego."

The Chargers had their first lead of the game, with only thirty-five seconds left.

"What happened?" I shouted.

"She got too close to the fireplace and brushed her hand against the grill," Lee Ann answered.

"I know that. I meant with the Chargers' scoring." I barked.

My agitated voice drew more tears out of Katy. Zack followed his sister's lead. Lee Ann turned her green eyes toward me. "You're better than that," she said. I felt a twinge of regret about a conversation we had on our wedding night, encouraging her to always stand up to me when she thought I was wrong, something my mother hadn't always done with my father, succumbing instead to his raised voice or the commanding presence of his hands parked on his hips.

I tried to gather my composure and added, "How bad is it?"

"The Dolphins are losing by a point now, 22–21," Lee Ann said.

"I know that. I meant Katy's hand. Do we need to go to the hospital?"

"No, I think she scared herself more than anything."

The Dolphins had half a minute to play catch-up.

Dan Marino completed a pass and called a timeout.

Twenty-five seconds left.

Marino went to the sideline to talk with Shula and my dad.

"What do they talk about?" Lee Ann asked, nodding to the TV. "I've always imagined it was inspirational speeches with great music in the background like in the movies."

"Hardly. Definitely no music. Shula will frame the situation. Twenty-five seconds. Dolphins need to get to the Chargers' thirty-yard line for a field goal attempt. One timeout remaining. Try to save it for the field goal. It's part of Shula's genius. He can block out everything but the essentials."

"You mean he doesn't hear children crying?" Lee Ann asked.

"Probably not his entire life."

Marino completed another pass, but he had to use the final timeout before he got the Dolphins in field goal range. He had time for one last sideline conference.

"There's Pop-Pop!" Katy shouted as the camera zoomed in to Marino, Shula, and my dad.

"That's the goddamnit look," I said.

"Daddy—" Katy began. Lee Ann shushed her before she could finish.

"What's Marino saying?" Lee Ann asked.

"The play he wants to run. Big John will let him know any adjustments to make for the pass protection he'll need. Shula will say go with it or he'll change the play."

The fireplace spit and sizzled as the last flames died out. The four of us sat on the blanket in front of the TV, holding hands. Lee Ann's thin eyebrows rose in an arch of suspense. Marino completed a pass to put the Dolphins at the San Diego thirty-one-yard line with four seconds left.

"Stop the clock," I yelled.

Zack and Katy clung to Lee Ann.

The Dolphins field goal team sprinted onto the field for a chance to win the game.

The kicker, Pete Stoyanovich, lined up for a forty-eight-yard field goal attempt.

Four seconds left.

If Stoyanovich makes the kick, the Dolphins would go to the AFC Championship Game, one win away from the Super Bowl; if not, the Dolphins' season would end, and my father's career with it.

The TV showed the Dolphins' sidelines. Dad next to Shula. The shadows of sunset draped across their shoulders.

The center snapped the ball, and the game clock, shown in the upper right-hand corner of the TV screen, clicked down from :04 to :03 . . .

The holder put the ball down.

. . . :03 to :02 . . .

Stoyanovich kicked the ball.

. . . :02 to :01 . . .

"Kick on the way," Enberg said.

I held my breath.

The ball rose above the outstretched hands of the San Diego Chargers defenders.

The kick had a chance. Dad had a chance.

Then the ball wobbled into an unsteady flight. It veered off course. It fell short. No good.

:00

The ball, along with my father's hopes, came to rest on the grass in the end zone next to the shadow of the goal post.

The TV cameras turned their attention to the Chargers' celebration. They didn't show my dad slowly pulling off his headset and walking toward the locker room. But I could see it. I had taken that trip with him enough times. His broad shoulders slumping, his stride slowed to a toddle. His dark eyes cast down at the torn-up grass that slipped beneath his wide feet. A long, slow exhale.

Game day had ended, forever.

I clicked off the TV and felt the day's hope drain away. Katy gave me a hug and whispered in my ear, "It's okay if you want to say more bad words now, Daddy."

❧

For my father, retirement, like so much of his life outside of football, revolved around the social life of church. He helped count the money from the Sunday collections, sang in the choir, and became the de facto handy man and errand runner for the church school, where Shirley taught. He even volunteered to help the coaches at a new Catholic high school west of Hollywood, Archbishop McCarthy, which had just begun a football program.

The NFL had returned to Baltimore when the Cleveland Browns morphed into the Ravens. My fall schedule soon became as predictable and busy covering Ravens games as my father's had once been coaching in the NFL.

Lee Ann made a few trips a year to South Florida, taking Katy and Zack to see their pop-pop, even when work prevented me from joining them. And when I could make the trips I looked forward to long conversations next to the pool at his house while we watched the kids swim and play in his yard. Dad filled me in on Shirley and her three kids—Gina, Jason, and Jenny—now all through college with tuition he had gladly paid as the price to have a family surround him again.

Easter week, four years into my dad's retirement, a video game would give me the last glimpse of his football acuity. Zack brought his *Madden* video game to my father's house so he could play it on Pop-Pop's projector screen TV that stood five feet high and stretched at least that wide. It made the digital players appear nearly life sized. Zack and I played *Madden* half a dozen times a week, but this time he had a secret weapon—the coach. Zack sat at the foot of my father's leather recliner, tucked in between his pop-pop's thick, muscular legs. Prior to each play Zack scanned through the game's digital playbook of offensive plays and defensive formations, waiting for my father's cue. "That one," my dad would say, resting his hand gently on Zack's head, rubbing his mop of hair each time one of their plays tore through my defense for a twenty- or thirty-yard gain.

Katy pranced into the room and camped by me until our game turned into a rout. Laughing at my misfortune, she migrated over to the arm of my father's chair and snuggled up to her pop-pop, stretching her right arm as far as it could reach around his shoulders. My kids delighted in watching their pop-pop select the right formation, the right play, or the right defense every time. He even explained a few things to Zack: "Your father is panicking now. He gave up on his running game. Use a fake blitz and drop an extra man into coverage. That one. Two deep, man under. That's two safeties covering the deep part of the field and everyone else playing man-to-man coverage." Sure enough, my digital quarterback threw an interception that prompted Katy to kiss my dad on his cheek.

"Two deep, man under," Zack proclaimed, slapping high fives with his pop-pop.

I marveled at the soft touch my dad had with my kids. They gravitated to him, clung to him, loved him in ways I could have never imagined at their age. To them, he was a pillar made of marshmallow, big to the eye, soft to the touch. His voice, a soundtrack of fear to my childhood, was pitch-perfect folk hero to them.

On the final play of the game Zack scored a touchdown on a trick play my father had selected, bringing the final score to 70–7.

"Be careful, Pop-Pop. My dad uses bad language sometimes after football games," Katy said, making sure I saw how long her grin lingered.

"He better not," my dad bellowed, raising a clenched fist in the air.

Katy and Zack clung to my father, egging him on with their laughter, a burst of joy tapering off into long exhales.

"The old man's still got it, huh?" my dad said.

He did, but not for much longer.

In January Lee Ann and I flew to South Florida to help celebrate my dad's seventy-fifth birthday with a surprise party Shirley had arranged at the church hall. Jim and Ruth Ann came too, along with dozens of friends, coaches, and former players. Jack couldn't make the trip because of a work conflict.

My father thought he was going to choir practice.

He plodded along the concrete walkway leading to the church hall. His pace had slowed considerably in retirement. His feet, once so light on a football field and a dance floor, now seemed to sink in with each step as though he walked on wet cement. Old age had settled on him. His skin had an ashy look to it, his face more jowly than I remembered from my last visit. The traces of a limp had returned, as one of his artificial hips starting to wear out. "I'll just live with it," he had said when I asked him months earlier about another surgery. "You know how hard that was. I wouldn't put Shirley through that."

As he reached for the church door, Ruth Ann pushed it open and greeted him with a smile and a hug that disarmed and disoriented him. He looked up from Ruth Ann's shoulder and for an instant stared at Jim and me the way he looked at neighbors who lived on the far end of his street, people he recognized but didn't know, people who prompted a head nod but no verbal exchange.

"What in the hell are you doing at choir practice?" he asked, just as the lights turned on in the hall and the crowd behind us shouted, "Surprise!"

Don Shula stepped forward, along with Dan Sekanovich, Carl Tasseff, Dan Marino, Don Strock, and several of my father's former offensive linemen: Dwight Stephenson, a Hall of Fame center; Larry Little, a Hall of Fame guard; Bob Keuchenberg, Eric Laakso, Mark Dennis, Keith Simms, Richmond Webb, players from the seventies, eighties, and nineties, all mixed in with choir members, church ushers, neighbors, and friends.

My dad stood still for a few seconds, his mouth open, his eyes darting from side to side behind his glasses, surveying the situation the way he had done a thousand times on a practice field, making an assessment of what went wrong on a running play that lost two yards.

"Jesus," he said, breaking into a huge grin. "I guess this means there's no choir practice tonight."

Within a minute he had his favorite drink in his hand, a Manhattan, a cocktail of whiskey, sweet vermouth, and bitters over crushed ice. Before long he was singing Irish ballads and recounting half a century of football memories. A conversation with Don Shula revealed their shared irritation with San Francisco 49ers coach Bill Walsh for taking credit for creating the West Coast Offense. "Total bullshit," my father said, holding court at the end of a long, wooden table.

"Paul Brown started it in the fifties," Shula chimed in.

They had both played for the Cleveland Browns under head coach Paul Brown in the 1950s and still revered the man, even if they didn't much care for playing for him at the time.

"He could be a son of a bitch," my father said.

"So could we," Shula laughed.

"Walsh coached with him in Cincinnati, and the next thing you know Walsh invented the West Coast Offense."

"Horseshit. He gave Paul's offense a new name," Shula added.

Out of nowhere pen and paper appeared, and my dad and Shula were diagramming for Jim and me the Browns' short passing game from the fifties, with Otto Graham as quarterback, and comparing it to the one the 49ers had used to beat the Dolphins in Super Bowl XIX.

As the night progressed, other conversations with my dad revealed a lack of crisp recall, much like in the instant he had a vague stare when looking at Jim and me. For instance, I was standing with my father at a buffet table, and Lee Ann began cutting a sheet cake after my dad had blown out an armada of candles, when Dan Marino asked my father how long he had coached in Philly before going to the Dolphins.

My father returned a headshake and a squint as I slipped a piece of cake onto his paper plate. "I think I played there a couple of years after college," he said before walking back into the maw of well-wishers. He had misplaced everything about Philly, where he had coached, not played, nearly a quarter of a century after college.

"Three years," I said to Marino. "Seventy-three to seventy-five." *How did that slip past my father*? I thought.

I looked at Lee Ann, who had seen the exchange too. She shrugged her narrow shoulders and cocked her head to the side, a playful expression she used to remind me to have fun and worry less.

Dwight Stephenson, one of the best players my father ever coached, asked my father whether he was going to keep helping out the high school team at Archbishop McCarthy, something he had done since retiring from the Dolphins. It gave my father a semblance of a schedule in the fall: Practice at 3:30. Games on Friday nights. Beers with the coaches after the games.

The jowls that had spilled below my father's jaw line drooped further as he whispered, "No. The doctor won't let me anymore."

Doctors were like priests, generals, and head coaches—all authority figures he didn't question. He went on to explain that during McCarthy's last game in November one of the players had collided with him on the sideline and gouged a deep cut that required seventeen stitches on my father's calf. Then an infection slowed the healing. My father's doctor worried that another collision would have worse consequences. I worried that removing football completely from his life would cut far deeper than a flesh wound, a wound that stitches and Betadine would never heal.

It didn't take long to see my concerns play out.

After the party Lee Ann and I went back to Dad and Shirley's house to help move tables and chairs from the party back into their garage. Exhausted from the night, my father settled into his recliner while Lee Ann, Shirley, and I carried boxes filled with leftover food into the kitchen. On my last trip from the car I found my father staring at the wall above the blank television shouting, "Get out. Now. Out." At first I thought he was talking to me.

"Did I do something to upset you, Dad?"

"No, these goddamn little guys," he said, waving his hand in the air. "They knock on the door. They run through the house. They move shit around. Usually if I shout, they leave. There's one. Get out. They're quick bastards." He waved his hand again as though to dismiss the entire episode, and within a minute snoring replaced his strange rant.

Lee Ann found me standing in the kitchen, frozen by what I had seen.

"Are you okay? You look like you saw a ghost," she said, taking the cardboard box filled with unused plates and napkins out of my hand.

I had seen something far worse.

Because I had to travel to Tampa at the end of the week to cover the Super Bowl, Lee Ann and I extended our stay in South Florida a few days to spend more time with my dad. I took him to a bookstore in Hollywood to indulge in our shared passion for reading and to stock up on some of his favorite mystery writers—Robert Ludlum, Ken Follett, Morris West. I left him in the fiction aisle while I went to the magazine section. When I returned fifteen minutes later I found him exactly where he stood when I had walked away, statue-still, staring at a row of books, his eyes dark round sponges, soaking up the fluorescent light.

"Find anything you like?" I asked.

"Any what?"

"Books."

"No."

"Do you want to look at the large-print section?"

"Large-print what?"

"Books."

"No."

Before I could ask him if he was okay, he saw the *Writer's Digest* magazine in my hand and asked me whether I was still writing in my journal every day. Our conversation found a natural rhythm again, but his trancelike stare that seemed to detach him from time rattled me, give my chest a quick shake of a tambourine. My worry would multiply as the day continued.

After we went to lunch, as we drove west on Sheridan Street through Hollywood, heading back toward his house, my dad brought up my sister.

"Have you talked to Ruth Ann lately?"

"You mean since your party the other night?"

He stared at me a second too long, his eyes dull and blank. Then he turned his attention out the window without saying a word as we drove past rows of royal palm trees that stood like sentinels on both sides of the road.

His memory skip brought back something Ruth Ann had said to Jim and me after the party: "I think we caught Dad a little too much by surprise tonight. He never quite got his bearings after the surprise. Did you notice that?"

Jim nodded. "Let's face it," he said, "he was usually so busy, life's details didn't always catch his attention. Seemed like he had a great time."

"Absolutely," Ruth said. "I just meant, I don't know, he seemed a little turned at times. I asked him about Bob and Ginny, the old neighbors across the street in Cooper City, and he thought he had lived near them in New Jersey. There were a couple of things like that."

"Might have been the Manhattans too," Jim said.

Now, as I continued to drive with my father, I tried to soften the silence, nudging the conversation toward football.

"Do you still stop by the Dolphins' training facility once in a while?"

"Shirley takes me over every so often. I really don't like to drive near there. Too much traffic."

I knew it bothered him to feel like an outsider in a place he had worked for a quarter of a century. Two years earlier, on a visit to South Florida, Zack and I took my Dad to a Florida Marlins baseball game. They played in the same stadium as the Dolphins. Eager to show Zack where his pop-pop had coached, we walked through the entrance the Dolphins used at the stadium. (Jimmy Johnson had replaced Don Shula as the Dolphins' head coach three months earlier.) One of the guards recognized my father, but all of the photos of Don Shula and my father on the sidelines that had once hung in the lobby had been replaced with photographs of Jimmy Johnson and his assistant coaches. A new era had begun. Memories of the old era had been purged. My father had always seemed like such a permanent figure, but his imprint had been lifted as quickly as it took a team of overall-clad stadium workers to redecorate a lobby.

My father sensed how off balance the experience left me. Midway through the baseball game he casually said, "It's all temporary. You just have to enjoy what you have while you have it. Kind of like days like this." He had a broad smile as he looked over at me with my arm draped around Zack's shoulder.

Now something had started to remove his memories, stripping them from his mind the way the photos of him were stripped from the walls at the Pro Player Stadium.

Three years later the Dolphins had changed head coaches for a second time since my father retired. Dave Wandstadt had replaced Jimmy Johnson. Most of the players had changed too. During that season, when we talked each week on the phone, my father seemed to follow the team closely, sharing insights on who did and didn't play well. But now, as we drove through the heavy stretch of tourist season traffic, I remembered feeling jolted by a phone conversation we had near the end of the regular season about Dolphins defensive end Jason Taylor, a tall, slender player with a flair for sacking quarterbacks.

"If you were creating a game plan, how would you block Jason Taylor?" I asked.

"Let him get up field and run inside him. He's not stout enough to play the point of attack," Dad had said. "You have to account for his quickness."

"Is he a quality guy?"

"Who?"

"Jason Taylor?"

"Who?" Dad asked, as though he had never heard of the guy, much less outlined a block scheme for him eight seconds earlier.

"Number ninety-nine," I said. "Jason Taylor. Dolphins defensive end," I added.

"Who does he play for?"

"The Dolphins," I said.

"Are they playing today?"

"Dad, it's a Wednesday."

"I know what day it is."

When that phone conversation had skidded off topic, I had shrugged it off to static in the phone or something distracting my father, maybe Shirley shouting to him from the kitchen. But now, with yet another conversation mired in a dense cloud of silence and confusion, this one as thick as the South Florida traffic that surrounded my rental car, I felt a twinge of panic, the unsettled feeling of carbonation sinking deeper and deeper into the lining of my stomach. Something was wrong. I couldn't ignore it. Just then my sister saved me with a phone call.

"What's that?" my dad asked.

"My cell phone."

"Those things," his voice dripped with amazement. To my dad cell phones ranked up there with men walking on the moon. No cords—how did the damn things work? Ruth Ann had a similar concern about Dad's inconsistency. Traffic had started to move again. I handed Dad the phone.

"Hello? Hello?"

He handed it back.

"Ruth, you there?" I asked.

"Yeah. Is he okay?" She sounded as worried as I felt.

"Probably not. Let's try this again." I handed him the phone a second time.

Dad held the phone upside down and quickly grew agitated that he still couldn't hear Ruth. "I can't hear you!" He handed it back to me, and before I could adjust the phone to the right position, a car cut into my lane, nearly clipping my right fender. I swung the steering wheel to the left and hit the horn, dropping the phone.

"Shit!" I shouted.

"I couldn't agree more," my father chimed in. "Those damn cell phones never work."

Over the next several months, when I found myself on the other end of a phone call with my father, I felt him drifting farther and farther away. The blanks in his memory began to multiply along with the gaps in our conversation. The details that did come to mind for my father were mixed up chronologically, like asking me whether I was on my way to work at the TV station in Miami, where I hadn't worked for more than a decade.

Shirley was vague in what she shared with me about my father's visits to doctors. Lee Ann counseled me not to judge or to demand too much input. Shirley was his wife. She had signed up for better or for worse. Two words from my father more than fifteen years before— "I do"—had settled any debate over who would make health care decisions. I had walked with him during the darkest days of his life, but now, even I was becoming a lost memory, with my name and the sound of my voice taking longer to register with each call, bringing me fewer and fewer of the joyful lilts in his voice I treasured when he would say, "Hey, how are you, buddy?"

By the time he had a clear diagnosis of Alzheimer's, the disease had pilfered more than memories. It had stolen the effervescent side of his personality too. The walls of his life contracted, a shrinking perimeter of a prison. He stopped going to Dolphins reunions. It embarrassed and frustrated him to forget the names of so many people he had known and worked with for years. The words to songs disappeared, as though written with vanishing ink. Choir practice disappeared too.

When I called him with the sad news that Johnny Unitas had died of a heart attack, my father broke into tears, then sobs. I could hear his chest rising and falling as he tried to catch his breath. Shirley's voice, high and shrill, came on the phone. "Why is he so upset?" she demanded.

When I explained, she said my father couldn't get back on the phone. I don't think Shirley even knew who Johnny Unitas was or what he meant to my father.

"Tell him I'll call him tomorrow when he feels better," I said, equally mad at Shirley and myself—Shirley for trampling on what she didn't understand, me for failing to finesse such news my dad shouldn't have to hear about on some random sports show.

When I called my dad the next day I glimpsed the only positive of his condition. He had no recollection of talking to me the day before, what we talked about, or the death of Unitas. The onset of Alzheimer's erased painful memories too. Somewhere in my father's receding thoughts, Johnny Unitas still lived.

— Chapter Ten —

THE BLANK STARE

Before my father saw the end of his seventy-fifth year, his memories of his party had recoiled, burrowed in a crevice of his mind, inaccessible and lost. He tumbled into the gorge of Alzheimer's, confused, the tangle of time twisted around him, an invisible cord binding him to his recliner. Minutes, hours, days, weeks, months, years all blurred together. I called my dad more often, hoping our conversations would help stave off the erosion of his memories, but our phone conversations grew shorter as his attention and interest waned. He kept the phone within reach of his recliner, but he stopped answering many of my calls when the little people were darting through his house.

Each February a work trip to South Florida to cover the Baltimore Orioles spring training camp in Fort Lauderdale gave me a window of time to visit alone with my dad, a slice of time that belonged to just us. The first few years after he retired we would go out to lunch, visit an old neighbor, make a day of it together, drive around to nowhere in particular, all the while relishing the boundaries the car gave us. Me and him. No one else, especially not Shirley.

Shirley didn't understand my history with my father. She didn't know that Johnny Unitas wore number nineteen, that my dad always cooked kielbasa and eggs on Easter morning, that the first time I ate macadamia nuts he and my mom had brought them home from the Pro Bowl in Hawaii, and everyone in our family still thought about Dad and Mom and Hawaii every time we saw macadamia nuts. It wasn't Shirley's fault; she wasn't there. But it also meant every conversation around her got interrupted with a dozen explanations of things my father and I took for granted. That Bud Grant had coached in four losing Super Bowls with the Minnesota Vikings. That my father's signing bonus to his first NFL contract was a steak dinner. That we called his brother Uncle Moozer. That my parents met on a blind date. That Memorial Stadium in Baltimore was on 33rd Street and referred to as the world's largest outdoor insane asylum.

So when Shirley was around, conversations tended to feel more like interrogations. "Who is Mike McCormick? What's a nickel defense? What's the big deal about Super Bowl III? When did Don Shula play for the Colts?

I should have had more patience. After all, she hadn't lived our life, but a part of me, a part buried too deeply to locate and name, thought that also meant she shouldn't act like she was a seamless continuation of my dad's life, a natural progression from my mother to her. As time went by she asked fewer questions, I gave fewer answers, and we saw my father from different shores of the same river.

But by the time he had turned seventy-eight my father confided in me that he didn't feel safe anywhere but in his family room. And even there he had his torment: the little people.

Dad leaned forward in his leather chair and drew his hand back in a fist. "Get out of here!" he shouted, his agitation rising to anger as he shifted his weight to the front of his chair.

No one was there.

He relaxed his fist, pushed himself back in his chair, and laid his hands on the armrests. "They come and go," he said, as though explaining a seasonal weather pattern to me. "Usually when I shout they leave."

He no longer used the swimming pool in his backyard. Not twenty feet from his reclining chair, the pool lurked neglected and forgotten, like his old Dolphins, Eagles, and Colts playbooks that sat somewhere in his garage, buried beneath a metal Craftsman toolbox, sagging cardboard boxes filled with old clothes, a tack of press board, the flotsam and jetsam of forgotten projects.

Time had begun to rob my father of the glory of his size too. He no longer looked like Big John, the intimidating, monolithic figure who had scared me for all of my childhood. His arms, once beefy and powerful, had grown thinner and fleshy. His hair, black into his early seventies, had finally grayed and grown wispy, flyaway hairs falling against his forehead. His neck resembled an artist's crosshatch sketch, a collection of deep-cut lines, a lingering reminder of thousands of hours spent on practice fields in the midday sun. A trip to the bathroom had become a treacherous journey for him across a Mexican-tile floor with the help of an aluminum walker I feared might fail him if he slipped.

Shirley rebuffed any suggestion of putting her career on hold to care for my father. She was now a principal of a Catholic school. How would anyone praise her for standing up to the burden she faced if she actually spent all of her time facing the burden? She hired full-time help, a Venezuelan woman named Maudie who spoke little English but treated my father, whom she called "Meester Jhun," with a gentleness I remembered my mom showing him—a hand on his shoulder when she asked whether he wanted a turkey sandwich for lunch, a smile that settled comfortably across her small mouth, unforced and unfatigued as he stared at her, his lips unable to find the shape to sound out her name.

Shirley returned home in the evening, dropping her purse and a stack of files on the kitchen table with an exaggerated sigh as she dropped into a wooden chair at the kitchen table and asked Maudie for a glass of wine.

"How was your day, John?" she asked with exaggerated volume, before turning to me and whispering the same question.

"We, uh, we did, uh," my father began, his voice tinny and quivering, the sound of an old car radio loose in the dashboard. He paused, pursing his dry lips, his frustration turning inward at his inability to converse.

"What, John? What? What are you trying to say?" Shirley said, rolling her eyes as she turned her attention to me to talk about my father in a sugary tone of voice more suited to a puppy. "He's so sweet, isn't he? My man. It's so difficult, but I love him."

Her voice, heavy with contrived concern, infuriated me. I wanted to take my father home with me to Baltimore, but I knew that, shy of kidnapping, I had no way to do that. He was no longer the coach, but he was still Shirley's trophy, the symbol of her great struggle as the hard-working Catholic school principal. I suspected if I broached the subject of a better life for my father in Baltimore, Shirley could easily arrange for him to be at a doctor's appointment for every one of my future visits to South Florida. I also knew that in Baltimore a cold winter would add to the confusion of his shrinking world. I could share with him my home, but I would also confine him to a different type of exile, one divorced from the last images of familiarity: the long, dark hallway that led from the kitchen back to their bedroom where each day began and ended; his big-screen TV; the rectangular wooden table by the right armrest of his recliner that held a cordless phone and two mason jars, one filled with brown, red, and green M&M's, the other with small Reese's peanut butter cups wrapped in gold foil.

Sitting next to him, as my visit drew to a close, I felt as trapped by his circumstances as he did by his condition. Ruth Ann, Jim, Jack, and I had spoken about it at length. We were no longer talking about the dad who had recently buried Mom. He now belonged as much to Shirley as he belonged to us. He had made that choice. We had to honor it, not like it. Jack was the one who had shown me that.

Every year for Christmas Dad bought us a family dinner. We rotated who picked the restaurant and turned in the bill to Dad. The previous year Jack had picked the Prime Rib, an old Baltimore restaurant with white tablecloths and waiters in tuxedos. Jack couldn't have selected anything farther from his own personality. Jack was five feet, eight inches tall, a good five inches smaller than Dad. He had thick, jet-black hair that he still wore longer than my Dad would have ever imagined doing.

We had all arrived at the restaurant as interested in finding out why Jack picked it as we were in the menu. He said that as a kid the place had always reminded him of Dad—an icon, a fixture, a force so big it didn't have to change.

"But Dad has changed," Jack said, chuckling. "We all have. And no I wouldn't want to go back to the old ways. We hardly ever saw eye to eye on anything. I couldn't have been less like Dad, less like this place. But sometimes thinking about the way things were helps remind you that they aren't that way anymore. And that's not all bad."

Jack was the son who shared the fewest traits with our father and the son who was the most accepting of the choices Dad had made. He ran his fingers through his hair, revealing the faintest outline of a scar that lingered on the left side of his forehead where a car accident thirty years earlier had launched him through a windshield. Time fades most things, even differences.

The following Christmas Shirley let us know that even with full-time help, she couldn't manage with my father. She was putting him into an assisted-living home in Sunrise, about forty minutes from their house. This move added layers of complications to connecting with him. He didn't have a phone in his room—the ringing confused him. To talk with Dad I had to call the front desk. A staff member had to take the phone to my dad and assess whether he could talk. Most of my calls began with the sound of soft-soled shoes padding across a concrete pavement courtyard leading to Dad's room. "John? John? Would you like to take a phone call? John?" Most of my calls ended with a disappointing "I'm sorry. He doesn't seem up for it today."

After the football season—the season that once limited how much time my father could spend with me and now limited how much time I could spend with my him—Jim, Ruth Ann, and I flew to South Florida to see what we knew would become our father's last home. Sunshine poured into the open-air courtyard at the assisted-living facility as we made our way toward Dad. He was hunched over his aluminum walker, inching in our direction. Dad looked at us with a blandness that matched the beige stucco wall beside the walkway.

His brown eyes had a glassy emptiness, a stare no longer capable of sharp focus. Tufts of black hair grew from his ears like crabgrass on a neglected lawn. The skin on his forearms looked blotchy and brittle.

Careful not to startle him, the three of us waited for Dad to reach us. Even as we stood within an arm's length of him, he continued to look down at the sidewalk, shuffling a few inches with each step.

"Hi Dad," Ruth Ann whispered.

He slowly raised his eyes and looked at us. He scrambled for words, his lips, dry and cracked, trying on shapes with no sounds passing through them. Finally a raspy whisper rose from his throat, words none of us could decipher.

"It's your kids, Dad." Jim said. "Jim, Ruth, and Gerry."

Dad stared at us with no more sign of recognition than if he had come across three people who had taken an algebra class with him at South Philly High sixty-five years ago.

"Lunch," Dad mumbled. Then he lowered his head and continued scraping his feet along the concrete walkway in the direction of the dining hall. After he took a few steps Dad stopped and looked up at Ruth, making his first connection to our visit. She melted into his small, crooked smile and his outstretched arms.

At lunch we sat with Dad while he mechanically ate a grilled cheese sandwich and bowl of tomato soup, raising each spoonful to his mouth with the same exaggerated slowness of his shuffles behind his walker, each spoonful bringing with it a new discovery.

After lunch we accompanied Dad back to his room. Along the way we walked past a woman with a hunched back who also used a walker. My father exchanged grunts with the woman, not words or eye contact. Neither paused. Both inched by each other in a slow, methodical rhythm of trudging along with a walker—lift, lean, lower, shuffle, lift, lean, lower, shuffle—the cadence of movement in my father's world now. The awkward intersection peeled back my presumptions, exposing the flaws in my hopes that assisted living might give my father a sense of companionship, of shared experience. Alzheimer's victims aren't passengers on the same ship who get lost together; they get lost alone and simultaneously.

Back in his room each of us ran through family updates, enough to make us feel like good parents and good children at the same time.

A tear, then a stream made its way along Dad's ruddy cheek.

"Are you okay, Dad?" Ruth Ann asked, her hand resting on his blotchy forearm.

Sunshine slipped through the venetian blinds behind Dad, framing him in a soft golden backlight as his mood shifted, reflecting the dark shadow his body cast on the Berber carpeting. A stack of neglected novels and magazines sat on the nightstand next to him along with his familiar mason jars of M&M's and Reese's peanut butter cups. An old media guide from the 1985 Dolphins team rested on top of the pile. The orange, teal, and white cover of the dog-eared media guide looked as tired and outdated as Dad.

We sat quietly watching our father lie down on his bed, close his eyes, and retreat to the safety of sleep. We knew that when Dad woke to a knock on his door, announcing dinner, the memory of our visit would be as far from him as the man in the seven-paragraph biography recalling the pinnacle of his youth as an All-American tackle at Villanova as well as a long and distinguished NFL career in the neglected media guide an arm's length away.

Over the next few months my phone calls led to little more than an attendant's walk to my father's room with my hopes for a short conversation in his hand, followed by an apologetic "not today."

On a Friday night in late April, when my job took me to the Hippodrome Theatre to serve as master of ceremonies of the Miss USA preliminary pageant, I called my father, hoping to share even the tiniest thread of connection. After the attendant's prodding, my father answered with the temerity of a child seeking forgiveness for something he had done wrong.

"Dad, it's Gerry," I said. I would settle for him recognizing my voice, but I hoped I could bring him a smile too. "You'll never guess where I am."

"Are you here?" he asked.

"No, still in Baltimore."

"Who is this?" His voice was weak, distant, disconnected.

"It's Gerry. Your son. I just called to tell you what I'm doing at work today."

I heard only the sound of my dad's labored breathing, but I continued to tell him about my night. I served as the show host for fifty Miss USA contestants in the preliminary judging round. Backstage, clouds of hairspray congealed like smog as mothers and makeup artists fussed with contestants' hair. Producers wearing headsets, similar to the ones NFL coaches wear on the sidelines, scurried through narrow hallways calling for sheet music and for contestants to line up for dance numbers.

"Two, three, four, turn, and two, three, four, turn," the show's director barked at the contestants as they preened across the polished wood stage during rehearsals.

"Second turn, Gerry, that's where you have to wrap up your read and punch it with the contestant's state name. Miss MINNESOTA! Got it?"

I nodded to the director, a tall man with a wiry build and a ponytail that swung behind him as his attention darted around the stage. After rehearsal I returned to my dressing room, complete with a star on the door and a placard that read, "Gerry Sandusky" beneath the star.

I recapped everything for my dad, pausing on occasion in case he had a question or a comment but also to listen for his breath to make sure he hadn't set the phone down or walked away from it, shuffling with his walker to the bathroom.

"The show doesn't begin for another two hours, Dad. I wish you were here. You were always better at talking to pretty women than I was. I could still use a few pointers."

I laughed but heard nothing in return other than his shallow breath scratching through the phone. I was a little disappointed, but still, that was my dad's breath. He had stayed on the line. I held onto that, treasured it the way I treasure the last hours of a beach vacation, the sunset warm against the back of my neck, my gaze set on the waves falling on the empty beach in front of me, a scene I know I will miss, just as I already missed my dad.

"Well, I'm going to get going now. I love you, Dad."

"Okay," he said, more of a two-syllable mumble than a word. I hit the end button on my cell phone and turned my attention to my empty dressing room. The awareness that I could no longer share any experience with my dad settled on me, a heaviness pressing down on my shoulders, the clunky feeling of wearing shoulder pads on the first day of training camp, their plastic layers clattering with each step you take. He was out of reach. A knock on the door held off an assault of sadness.

A young woman wearing a headset and holding a clipboard stood at the door. "We're serving a buffet in the Meyerhoff Room," she said. "If you would like, I can take you there, Mr. Sandusky."

"That's sweet of you," I said. "But there's still only one man who answers to Mr. Sandusky. I'm only his son."

When Halloween arrived, along with the chill of fall in Baltimore, Lee Ann, wearing a tall, black witch hat, tinkered with the finishing touches to Zack's costume, a furry mouse. She had decorated the front of the house in fake cobwebs and placed carved pumpkins with flickering candles inside on the front porch. I smeared eye black, the kind football players wear under their eyes, on Katy's cheeks to complete her hobo outfit. For our kids Halloween was a destination in itself, but to me it still brought memories of seeing the day as a measuring stick. The NFL season bridges five holidays: Labor Day, Halloween, Thanksgiving, Christmas, and New Year's Day. In a coach's family each holiday serves as a mile marker on the journey of a season. Labor Day ushers in the start of the new season. By Halloween you know whether your father's season has started well. At Thanksgiving playoff chances come into focus. Coach's kids hope their father works a long day on Christmas because it means his team has either made the playoffs or needs one more win to do it. On

New Year's Day, if your father's team remains alive, the only thing you talk about is winning the Super Bowl.

Now, as the foot traffic of princesses, Ninja Turtles, Darth Vaders, and vampires started to arrive at our front door, Lee Ann sensed my pensiveness.

"Should I try to call him?" I asked her.

"Take the kids around the neighborhood. I'll hand out the candy at the door."

She was right. She had put a lot of effort into Halloween, including finding a shade of nail polish with an exotic name, something like peat-smoked salmon, that she and Katy shared, laughing together that only Katy would be a perfectly accessorized hobo for Halloween. My wife and children deserved my focus. As Katy and Zack pulled on my hands, leading me through the front door, we passed a boy cleverly dressed as an ear of corn. And I remembered feeling the anticipation my children had right now, the racing heartbeat, the urge to tap your feet while counting down the hours, then the minutes until sharing a long-awaited night with your father. My night, when I was their age, always came in late August on family day, near the end of Baltimore Colts training camp.

We made the drive through winding country roads in Carroll County, Maryland, past rolling cornfields, and we knew training camp neared its end because golden tassels crowned each corn stalk as though Nature herself understood the rhythms of football season. My mom, brothers, sister, and I, sitting on a hillside that overlooked the practice field, would watch the Colts practice at Western Maryland College. And in the evening, after the coaches' sons played touch football on the grass in the quad in front of the dorms where the coaches and players stayed, we walked together as a family to the cafeteria for a dinner of fried chicken, fresh corn, and mashed potatoes.

"Some catch you made there, buddy," I remembered my dad saying one evening on our walk to the team cafeteria. His huge hand mussed my hair, and he pulled me close to his enormous body, the smell of Ivory soap and Vitalis hair tonic mixing with the fresh-cut grass and August humidity. I leaned into my father, feeling the girth of his upper body, the power of his arms, and the full weight of his attention. I wanted nothing more than to figure out how to make time stand still.

Now, as I walked in front of our house and merged into a swelling tide of pirates, Power Rangers, and Barbies who filled the sidewalk, I reached out and drew my children close to me and silently thanked my dad for a lesson he never knew he taught me.

On my next trip to South Florida to see my father he confused me with my late brother Joe, and in a sliver of clarity he implored my brother Jim and me to live our lives now: "Don't wait. It's no fun at the end."

It was the last bit of wisdom we would ever hear from our father.

My third trip to my father's assisted-living home came shortly after his eightieth birthday. My brothers, Jack and Jim, and I went to see our dad, knowing that the day of the week, season of the year, time of the day would all mean nothing to him now. The chair outside of his room that looked out onto a rectangle of Bermuda grass in the courtyard sat empty. We found Dad sitting on the edge of his bed in his narrow, rectangular room with walls as blank and stripped down as his memory. He was frozen in a forgotten movement, unsure whether he was rising from or returning to a nap.

He stared blankly at us, his pupils unfocused beneath heavy eyelids. The attendant who had walked us to his room whispered that our father was having a lot of bad days lately. Dad's gray hair had thinned since my last visit. It looked too long on the sides and the back, his eyebrows bushy. I sat next to him, and he turned his face in my direction. He had dark beard stubble and stale breath. His skin sagged. Nothing registered in his eyes as he turned and looked at my brothers.

We had each in our own way spent plenty of time in our youth wishing, praying Dad wouldn't call us, wouldn't hear us, wouldn't see us. We knew then it might spark a lecture, a reprimand, an explosion. But now with our father having coasted beyond recognizing his sons, each of us digested that our father couldn't call us, couldn't hear us, couldn't see us—and never would again.

There was nothing any of us could say that would help our father now, so I drew on something he had taught me years before: sometimes sitting and saying nothing is the most important thing you can do for a person you love.

For me that moment came in eighth grade. The basketball team I played on at St. Jude's elementary school had made it to the Catholic League championship. We played the game after school on a Wednesday in February. My father had seen many of my games that season, the ones we played on Friday nights or Saturday mornings, but he wouldn't be able to make it to a four o'clock game on a workday. I understood that. We played St. Rose of Lima, a school a few towns north in what seemed like a far wealthier area than where I went to school in Blackwood, New Jersey.

I had never played in a championship before. I could feel my heart hammering as I went through pregame warm-ups, dribbling a basketball on the tile floor of a tiny gym in Haddonfield, New Jersey, that suddenly felt as large as the Spectrum, where the Philadelphia 76ers played. The best player on our team, a sharp-shooting guard named Mario Saponaro, led the league in scoring. Mario had a blocky build, thick black hair, side-burns, and the shadow of facial hair on his upper lip and chin that made him look two years older than everyone else on the team. For most of the season we just got the ball to Mario, and he found a way to score. But early in this game it became obvious that St. Rose's coach had designed a defense to prevent Mario from getting many shots. That defense left me open to shoot my favorite shot, a jumper from the corner. My first shot rattled around the rim and popped out. No good. My second shot clipped the inside of the front of the rim and skipped across the top of the basket. My third hit the front of the rim. My fourth, the back of the rim. My fifth missed everything. Somehow, without Mario getting shots and without me making shots, we still only trailed by two points at the start of the fourth quarter. I felt like someone had pulled a thick leather belt across my chest, squeezing out the air from my lungs and preventing me from drawing a deep breath. Each shot I took, raising the ball over my head, releasing the ball from my outstretched fingers, looked like it was on a perfect arc to snap through the net and pull us even. But each shot found a way to hit the rim, miss the mark, and leave my team trailing. I could feel the stares of disappointment from the bench, from the crowd, as I ran down the court, dragging dread with me, sweat trickling down my sides, dropping from one rib to the next, down to the sides of my stomach, where the urge to vomit had started to diffuse like a droplet of ink in a glass of water.

In the final minute of the game Mario managed to squeeze an off-balance shot through a crowd of defenders to pull us within a point. St. Rose's coach called a timeout with fifteen seconds left to play. On the inbounds pass Mario stole the ball. Three defenders converged on him. He dribbled frantically, his hands and the ball close to the floor, his eyes darting around the court, looking for an opening to the basket.

Eight seconds left.

The defense forced Mario back toward the half-court line.

Six seconds left.

Mario jumped and fired a pass to me in the corner along the baseline. My hands trembled as the ball arrived with a thunk.

Four seconds left.

I squared to take the shot that could win the championship. One shot—that's all I needed to make, a chance to redeem myself and wipe out the worst shooting game I had ever suffered.

Three seconds.

I jumped, raising the ball above my right eye and over my head.

Two seconds.

At the peak of my jump I released the ball, rotating it from the tips of my index and middle finger, the way I had done a thousand times in practice. All eyes turned to the ball, the basket.

One second.

The ball descended from its arc, the championship on the line.

The buzzer sounded.

My shot, the last shot of the season, the biggest shot of the season, hit the back of the rim and caromed long, falling to the floor along with our hopes of a championship.

By the time I made it home my Dad was sitting in the family room, watching TV. I walked into the room, and he greeted me with smile that flew from his mouth before his words. He knew what a championship game felt like. He had played in six of them in the NFL and coached in five. He knew about the adrenaline rush, the way time stood still, how the rest of the world vanished from the start of the game until the finish. "How did you do?" he asked in a voice so big I could feel his hopes wrapping around me like one of his bear hugs.

I opened my mouth, but a clot of emotions blocked my words. Tears poured down my cheeks. A sob rattled my shoulders. His eyes softened. His head nodded. He patted the empty seat next to him on the couch, and I walked over and sat down. My father put his arm around my shoulder, and for the next hour we sat there staring at the TV at an episode of *The Waltons*. Not a word passed between us. He didn't need any to convey that his understanding plumbed the depth of my discouragement. The side of his burley chest and the shelter of his arm and hand gave me safe harbor from my failure.

By the time *The Waltons* had ended with its signature volley of good nights, I rose from the couch to go to bed. My father looked me in the eyes and nodded, perfectly conveying that his disappointment was for me, not in me.

Now, as I sat next to my father on his bed, I hoped the warmth of my arm draped around his back might slip through the fog of Alzheimer's and numb his pain. I ran a comb through his hair, returning his neat part and returning to him a gift he had once given me: the gift of silent understanding that no moment—no matter how big, how painful—lasts forever, but a small tenderness can get you through, both that moment and the ones still to come.

— Chapter Eleven —

GOOD-BYE

By early spring my father's life had made a final shift from the black hole of Alzheimer's, where time has little relevance, to the tight squeeze of hours that would make one more thousand-mile journey a race against time to say good-bye.

After my sister called to tell me that Dad had gone to the hospital and it was serious, Lee Ann pulled together a flight and rental car for me in the time it took me to shower and dress. Before I knew it I found myself sitting in a window seat on a plane, staring out at wisps of clouds below and feeling turbulence unfold inside of me. I guided my thoughts to memories of my father, ones that had left indelible imprints on my senses. The thick, musty smell of sweat that followed him off the practice field. The ice-cold sweat trickling down my sides when my father greeted me at the front door after my sophomore year in college, holding a letter from the director of housing informing him that because I threw my furniture out of the window of my third-floor dorm room during a party that got wildly out of control I would not be welcomed back in the dorms the following year. (I'm still amazed he didn't punch me right then and there. He just stared at me, the disappointment as conspicuous as the letter he crumpled slowly in his right hand. I could still remember his hot breath hissing through clenched teeth as I squeezed past him in the doorway.) I remembered my flinch reflex too every time I saw a hammer raised in his hand along with his voice when we worked on a project, like trying to fix a sprinkler system that neither one of us knew anything about. The rich, deep sound of his voice belting out a verse of "Danny Boy." His effortless movement on a dance floor, the way he glided and spun my sister when they danced the jitterbug at her wedding, everyone standing around the parquet dance floor marveling at how a three hundred–pound man could make it seem his feet levitated just above the wood floor.

At Fort Lauderdale airport my thoughts quickened to the pace of evaporating time. I stood second in line at the rental car counter and called my brother Jim, who arrived on an earlier flight and already made it to the hospital.

"Hurry, there's not much time," he said.

I asked the man in front of me if I could go ahead of him because, my voice broke, and the reality of the end slipped through every invisible defense I had constructed, "I'm trying to get to my dad before he dies."

When South Florida traffic didn't cooperate with me, I ran red lights, each time thinking that when I was a teenager my father would have killed me if I got a ticket for ignoring a light. I guided my rental car onto the shoulder of the road to pass a woman in a slow-moving minivan, my thoughts rattling like the loose gravel the car moved across. This was the trip my father had wanted to make on the day Joe died. The trip he didn't get to make. The trip to say good-bye.

When I got to Coral Springs Medical Center I made my way down the long corridor that led to Dad's room. I wanted to sprint but could feel each step I took slowing, a counterbalance to my racing heart that beat so loudly it now drowned out my thoughts. Much like my father's final walk from a football field, this was my final walk to see him.

Jim and Ruth Ann greeted me near Dad's room with tear-soaked hugs and disjointed information, scraps of conversations they had with doctors and nurses that didn't really matter now.

Jack was on the next flight in. Would I like a little time alone with Dad?

My father was lying on his back on a hospital bed, metal railing pulled up on each side to prevent him from rolling off. His cheeks looked sunken and sallow. His eyelids fluttered. He ground his teeth. His stare pointed up at the ceiling, but his focus seemed far beyond the drop ceiling. He silently mouthed words to someone far beyond the eggshell colored walls of his hospital room.

I held his hand and felt him clench mine, the reach of a generation.

I couldn't tell whether he wrestled to hold onto life or to let it go, but as he tightened the grip on my hand, I smiled. My father still had the strength to wrestle angels or demons, whichever came his way.

When he grew still and his breath became shallow and labored, Dad looked me in the eyes. I leaned over and whispered in his ear, "I love you, Dad. I'll miss you." I paused and added, "Tell Mom and Joe I said hello."

He grew still, his breath ragged, and I remembered when I was a little boy, my father lying down on the living room floor in the evening, exhausted from his day. He would promise to pay me a quarter to scratch his back. It always felt like I rode an elephant into a circus, sitting on the small of his back, his massive frame rising and falling to the rhythm of his breath. If I stopped too soon or demanded my quarter, he would playfully begin to rise to all fours and demand I keep scratching or he'd be forced to squash me. I would return to scratching his back, all the while laughing. "Tell me about your day," my father would say. And before I had run through much of what occupies a six-year-old's day, his breath would grow shallow before adding the percussion of a snore.

Now, as I stood over my father, my hand on his, I knew he would never wake from his next sleep.

For so much of my life I had avoided telling my father things I considered important. I often didn't know how to bridge a silence and sometimes feared a poorly piloted attempt might veer into a disagreement or just a weighty awkwardness we would both rather avoid. I never told him how much I loved Lee Ann, how much her smile and the sight of her dark hair streaked with highlights could make me put aside my ambition, replacing it with the urge to do nothing more than drink up the scent of her soft skin. I didn't share with him how much I missed Joe, because I didn't want to add to his burden. I avoided mentioning how disappointed

I was for him that he never got a second shot at a head coaching job in the NFL. Invisible walls rise between a father and son, preventing us from sharing so many of the details that make our lives unique. We didn't discuss sex beyond the one time I asked him to extend my curfew when I came home from college after my freshman year and he insisted I still get home by midnight. He met my protest with, "If you can't get it done by midnight, you're not much of a man anyway." End of discussion. I never asked him how much money he made, and he never asked me. Those were questions that didn't need answers. We had a silent understanding. If I needed anything or if he needed anything, we would be there for each other. No questions asked.

There was one last thing I did want to share.

Following the 2005 Ravens season, the team switched its broadcast rights to WBAL radio, the sister station of the TV station I worked for. The switch brought me the career opportunity I had dreamed of since I once stood in an empty broadcast booth in the Orange Bowl as a twenty-two-year-old intern at a station in Miami. The play-by-play job for an NFL team. I had finalized the deal in late January but had no way to share the best news of my career with my father. He didn't take phone calls any longer. He didn't read letters. He knew nothing about e-mail. I knew that even now, standing next to him, I couldn't convey my excitement, but I also believed that somewhere beneath the blanket of confusion that muffled his exit from this life he could still hear with his soul, a soul that understood the power of dreams come true in a game that had meant everything to him, had formed the outline of his life.

I had known from my days of playing college football for a division II school, Towson University, that my future didn't include playing or coaching football. My father had seen enough of me running around training camps to know the same. Even my limited playing career involved more talking than anything else. On road trips I would sit in the back of the team bus and do mock interviews with my teammates about that day's game. Those evolved into a full-scale, albeit pretend, show we called "The Postgame Show" that would last for the duration of the bus ride back to Towson.

In a game at Central Connecticut, when we trailed by four points in the final minute of the game, I ran onto the field after the second-string tight end suffered an injury. I was the third-string tight end and presumed I would replace him. But by the time I reached the huddle our head coach, Phil Albert, had run on the field halfway to our huddle, waving his left arm like a windmill and yelling for me to get back on the sideline. Staring through the facemask of my helmet, I stood on the sideline, breath vapors rising in the chilly November air, and watched us score the winning touchdown, but I felt little desire to celebrate. On the bus ride back to Baltimore, when traffic congestion in New York slowed our progress through Brooklyn, I rose from the back of the bus during one of our fake commercial breaks on the Postgame Show and walked to the front of the bus, where I sought out Coach Albert to ask him why he didn't use me, with the game on the line and the second-string tight end injured?

Coach Albert answered without an instant of hesitation: "Because you aren't any good."

I took half a step backward, feeling like he had punched me in my chest. Then I followed with a second question: "Then why do you bring me on every road game if you don't intend on letting me play?"

"Because your teammates love that make-believe show you do. What do you call it?"

"The Postgame Show."

"Exactly. It makes the trip home go faster for everyone. Isn't your commercial break about done? Get back to doing your show before everyone else figures out that we're stuck in traffic."

I never shared that exchange with my father, not wanting to admit what I'm sure he already knew. I wasn't going to play football for a living. And a few years later, after graduating college, when I told my father I wanted to become a broadcaster—a career I had never taken a class to

prepare for—he nodded, letting me know I had made a good choice without asking what had prompted my decision.

Now my father was lying on a hospital bed, a crisp, white sheet pulled
up to his waist, his hands flinching involuntarily. We were alone for a last
time. I bent down and put my lips next to his ear and whispered through
fissures of pain, "Dad, I made it to the NFL too."

I hoped that our last moments together—when I did share my vulnerability and my excitement, my thrill as a professional, my pride as a
son—would give him a smile I wouldn't see but that he could travel with
on his way to what comes next.

He squeezed my hand a little tighter and gave me a grip to hold onto
for the rest of my life.

Fittingly, my father died on a Sunday, the day of the week that my
mother had died on, the day of the week that had always made him feel
most alive.

In the days that followed I learned more about my father from the stories I had never heard before than from the ones I remembered. At his view-
ing a nurse who had worked at Pembroke Pines Hospital, where my mother
had died twenty-one years earlier, sought me out. She had read in the paper
about my father's passing and wanted to share a story she was sure I didn't
know. She had piercing blue eyes, the kind that swallow your attention.

She asked me to step outside where it was quiet.

"I remember you from your visits to the hospital," she said, brushing
back a few loose strands of gray hair from her eyes. "I retired a few years
ago, and in all the years I worked there I never saw anyone quite like your
father. I thought you should know he did more than just go to the hospital every morning and every night," she said, her voice barely above a
whisper. "In the evenings he would sing to your mom. Love songs, ballads, old Sinatra songs, Irish lullabies. He always stayed until after your
mom fell asleep, making sure the sound of his voice traveled with her in
sleep. Not a night went by that he didn't sing your mother to sleep, even
on the last night of her life."

She reached out and took my hand in hers. "I saw a lot of people bury their loved ones over the years, but none with quite as much love as that. A few of us nurses would gather outside of your mom's room when your dad would sing. One of my colleagues said one night, 'I hope when I die I leave hearing a voice with that much love in it.' I thought you should know that about your father."

That insight pounded me in my chest, robbing me of breath, not merely for the tenderness my father shared only with my mother but for the arrogance it revealed in me. I had been so furious with my father at the time for not talking more with my mom at the end, for not having a living will in place, for not knowing how to help his wife die. In my youthful certainty I had raged at him, mostly in silence or behind his back, like a coward, because I could only see his flaws. I could see now how my righteousness must have added to his burden. But he didn't add to my sadness by pointing it out to me. He had shown me a father's unselfishness, giving me the space to make my own mistakes and learn about them in my own time. Through the perspective of a woman whose name I didn't even catch, I could see how much of my immaturity he had weathered, knowing he most likely wouldn't see the day when I fully appreciated his strength.

On the day we buried my father I stood at the back of a Catholic church in Hollywood, Florida, where a chill moved like a spider down my back. Incense wafted from the brass, lantern-shaped canisters carried by two altar boys. I recalled the smell from my childhood when I served as an altar boy at funerals. The family of the deceased always tipped the altar boys, a tradition I never understood but gladly accepted. Who would tip these kids today? My thoughts gravitated to the harbor of the trivial like who would arrange for the altar boys to leave with a twenty-dollar bill rather than to lift the lid on the idea that my father was in the casket.

Every seat in every pew, the wood-backed benches that spanned from one aisle to the next, was filled. People stood along the back of the church. Dan Marino and his wife sat in the front row on the side of altar.

Don Shula and his wife, Mary Anne, sat a row behind the one reserved for family. The pallbearers, six of my father's former offensive linemen with the Dolphins, each one seemingly larger than the next, held the wooden rails on the sides of his coffin and began the slow walk to good-bye.

My family followed the casket down the church's middle aisle, Lee Ann at my side, her delicate right hand placed on the small of my back. I put one hand on Katy's shoulder, the other on Zack's. They had never been to a funeral before. I had been to too many, and my children needed only to glance at my puffy eyes to know what I had learned from my father: loss takes you to places words can't follow. Emotions with no names walk with you on the day you bury the people you love the most.

Near the end of the funeral mass I walked toward the altar to deliver the eulogy. My shiny black dress shoes clicked against the tile floor. I had polished my shoes the night before while I sat alone with my thoughts and tested my words to see which ones would stick like Velcro to my throat.

I stepped into the pulpit and looked at my father's casket. We had shared a thousand experiences during his life: from car rides to school to football games to long phone conversations. Today I had one last thing to share. I had something to say that I wished my father could hear.

Wrapped in the wooden arms of the pulpit, I continued to stare at my father's casket. It was draped in a ceremonial cloth that one of the priests had spoken about earlier in the service, something symbolic, of what I didn't know. The rote banter of a funeral mass had deflected off me like rain spattering off a tin roof.

I took a little strength from the choir, who sang with a conspicuous space left unfilled in the front row where my father had stood on Sundays, singing at mass until Alzheimer's had embezzled the words of his songs.

I looked out onto the gathering, feeling the quiver of emotion in each breath. I glanced at Lee Ann. She knew my struggle, but she also knew where I could draw my strength. She had reminded me of it when we woke that morning. "Be the point of the arrow," she had said. Now she nodded to me, putting the tip of her index finger to her lips and blowing me a small kiss. It was time to be the point of the arrow.

The phrase had come from an e-mail I received the day after my father died from a man named Larry Harris, a retired editor of a Baltimore newspaper. He shared with me a story about my father that I had never heard but would forever remind me of how my father faced impossible situations.

The Colts staff had coached in the 1967 Pro Bowl, which, back then, was still played in the cavernous LA Coliseum. After the game the locker room had cleared out except for a few: Johnny Unitas, the biggest star in the NFL; his friend, actor Jim Nabors; and this sportswriter, Larry Harris. My father, as was his way, had also remained in the locker room to ensure all the players got on their way home safely.

My father went to the locker room door, peered out into the tunnel, and returned with what Larry Harris recalled as a peculiar look on his face. "There must be a thousand people out there," my dad said. "They're all chanting for Unitas. And there aren't any police in sight."

"You can't go out there, John," Jim Nabors said, expressing the concern they all shared. "They'll tear you apart."

My father proceeded to organize what few resources he had available. "Okay," he said, "I'm on the point of this arrow we're going to make, and we're going to march through this crowd. Larry, you take the left side. Nabors, you're on the right. John, get in the middle, and hunker down a little. Everybody get your elbows out, use your luggage to protect you, and whatever you do, don't stumble or go down. You'll never get up again."

Larry Harris described what followed this way: "And with that, Sandusky strikes his best pass-blocking stance, and the phalanx starts out. He never says a word, just uses his mass to plow steadily ahead as hundreds of people scream, grab, and scratch, trying to reach Unitas. It is the longest walk any of us have ever taken, and I, for one, am terrified. At the end of the tunnel the crowd breaks up, and the beleaguered foursome reaches the safety of taxis. Inside the cab I take off my tattered shirt and throw it out the window and thank the heavens for Big John Sandusky. He just may have saved the lives of all of us."

My father had left me a final example of how to do more than stare at the impossible: be the point of the arrow.

And so I began.

"My name is Gerry," I said. "I am the fifth child."

My father had adopted all three of Shirley's children. He felt he had eight kids. I had been less generous in sharing our family name. But now, as I looked at each of Shirley's children, Jason, Gina, and Jenny, each grown and married, I could see tears shimmering on their faces. They would miss the big man as much as I would, as much as Jack, Jim, and Ruth would. I had always felt like my father had given away something precious, a piece of our name. Now, in the clarifying light of mourning, I could see my father's intention: he had expanded his heart, not diluted our name.

"I only saw or heard my father cry three times in my life: when my brother died, when my mother died, and when Johnny Unitas died.

"But I could always count on seeing him smile at three other times: on the first day of training camp, after mass—when he agreed with the sermon, when he got together with friends and the Manhattans and scotch flowed and they sang Irish songs. God, that man could sing.

"In the mix of those tears with those smiles you begin to see the outline of the value system that John Sandusky lived by: He loved his family. He loved his players. He loved his friends. He loved his faith. And he was loyal to them all."

I could feel a lump rising in my throat as I looked down to my eleven-year-old son. Zack was awestruck that such accomplished figures from the NFL had come to his pop-pop's funeral—Don Shula, Dan Marino, Bob Griese, Larry Little, Dwight Stephenson, and so many more. As I looked at my son brush back tears, I knew I had two jobs in front of me: say good-bye to my father and teach my son a lesson he could tuck away in emotional escrow until the day came when he would have to bury his father.

I went through the names of each of our family members and the thumbprints of influence Dad had placed on each of us. The simplicity of right and wrong. The importance of choosing right. Rise early and at full speed. Sing loudly. Live now.

"And since my father measured so much of the success of his life on the final score on Sundays, we should look at the final score on his life: eighty years; fifty-four wedding anniversaries; forty-three seasons in the NFL; twenty-six years working with Don Shula." I paused, looked at Coach Shula, and added, "Let's be honest here: that alone should get a man into heaven." Coach Shula gave me a gesture I had seen him flash players countless times: the fingers on his right hand clenched in a fist with the thumb resting against the knuckle of his index finger instead of tucked in front of it, a gesture of encouragement. Keep going. Finish strong.

"Nineteen months fighting in World War II; twelve grandchildren; eleven championships; eight children; five siblings; four Super Bowls he coached in; two wives; one Super Bowl ring. The value of spending any part of that experience with John Sandusky, priceless."

I spoke of Dad's pain over losing Joe at such a young age and the guilt he carried the rest of his life for not getting to Joe before he died. "So smile for my father today. For there is no more guilt. Dad, you finally made it to Joe.

"And so his life has come full circle. On his final day with us, in his final moments, the people who loved him most stood by his side as he took his final breath. In the remarkable silence of that moment we all stood there, holding his hands and his arms. We didn't say a word. We didn't have to. We knew that he knew that we love you, Dad. We all love you."

A few weeks after the funeral I answered a knock on the front door of our house. A FedEx driver needed my signature on a delivery.

I presumed it was for Lee Ann, as most packages that come into our house have her name on it. I didn't have my glasses on, so I set the package on the kitchen counter and went about my day, having no idea of the importance of its contents.

The arrival of spring in Maryland had brought with it a long list of chores and yard work. Since my father's death I had found it strangely therapeutic to put my hands in the dirt, clean up the gardens running along the side of our house, trim the hedges—tasks that brought me little more than a sense of obligation in the past. Today, cutting back an unruly hedge brought me sanctuary—alone with my thoughts, adjusting to the idea that from this point forward I was the front line of the living in my family. Working in the yard with my father had never brought me a sense of positive anticipation. Odd that now I find it to be the place where I can escape the usual pace and demands of my days. Time had taken on a strange shape for me since my father had died. Little things, like getting to work on time, seemed like a monumental task, a mountain climb that I lacked the appetite and energy for.

After puttering in the yard most of the morning with only scant evidence of accomplishment, I returned to the kitchen to have lunch with Lee Ann.

"A package came for you," I said, foraging through the refrigerator, looking for sliced turkey to make a sandwich. "I left it on the counter."

The buzzer on the washing machine sounded. "Make me a sandwich too?" she asked before walking to the basement to put the clothes in the laundry.

After lunch I returned to the garden, hoping a clear, sunny day would help me shed my lethargy, promising myself that even if I didn't feel like it, today I would push myself back to my old pace. Today I would let my feeling of loss follow me, not lead me.

When I came back inside to shower before going to work, Lee Ann brought a neatly folded stack of clothes up from the basement into the kitchen. "What did Shirley send you?" she asked.

"Me?"

"The package was addressed to you. Not me. It's from Shirley. You expecting something?"

I didn't expect to hear from Shirley again for the rest of my life. When we said our good-byes after the funeral I got the feeling she meant forever.

"Did we leave something at Dad's house?" I asked.

"Not that I know of."

"Whatever. I'll get to it after I shower. I'm running a little late for work."

"No. Open it now. I want to see what Shirley would send you," Lee Ann said. Over the years Shirley would occasionally send a random package, untethered from an obvious holiday or birthday, with a gift or two for the kids that either didn't fit or make sense, like a pair of dark blue pajamas decorated with the planets of the solar system, a gift Zack would have loved four years earlier.

"Babe, I really have to get going. I have a newsroom meeting today at three-thirty. I have to be out the door by three. As much for myself as anything."

Since my father's death I wrestled with time. I preferred to get lost in a project or just my thoughts and let time evaporate, and then I would scramble to return to the basic demands of each day—getting the kids to school on time, getting to a meeting on time. Since burying my father the desire to escape pulled at my attention stronger than calendars and clocks. His death had unmoored my bearings enough to make me wonder whether a daily TV sportscast or preparing for the NFL draft had really lost meaning or I had just lost my sense of direction.

"You've been walking around in a fog the past few weeks. Now suddenly you want to be mister on-time-to-work?" Lee Ann handed me the package. I took the tip of my car key and poked it through the brown tape on top of the box, when the doorbell rang again. A neighbor wanted to borrow cream. After retrieving the carton from the refrigerator I went upstairs to get a shower, leaving the unopened box on the kitchen counter. What could Shirley possibly send me that could make me feel better? Lee Ann had always explained the inconsistent arrivals of boxes with Shirley's name on them as her attempt to have a relationship with the kids. A feeling of relief at no longer having to pretend that I cared moved through me as I turned on the shower.

By the time I was ready to leave for work I felt the nudge of the clock that psychologists call eustress, the healthy push in the direction of fulfillment. I knew I had to embrace little things again—routines, the cadence of the ordinary. Even if I didn't want to or believe that it mattered, I had to push myself out of this malaise. Meetings don't matter after you bury someone you love. But finding a way out of my drift did matter. That's not who I am. Unfortunately, I couldn't find my keys. It was 2:58.

I looked in all the usual places: nightstand, pants I wore last, desk in the loft.

2:59.

My small step forward started to feel more like a tumble. I really have to pull it together.

"I found them," Lee Ann called. "They're in the kitchen."

3:00.

I could still make it to work on time. Maybe that would help. Maybe just pretending it mattered would help. And maybe it would keep me busy enough in the illusion of it mattering that I could escape the recurring grip around my throat that my dad was gone, a feeling that had caught me completely by surprise since his funeral.

When I made it to the kitchen Lee Ann held out the box Shirley had sent, my car keys jutting out from the top.

The meeting could wait.

I opened the box and read the letter inside.

"Gerry, your dad wanted you to have this. He made a point of it in his will. He thought it would mean the most to you, a way to remember all the good times you shared, not just the tough ones. Shirley."

I peeled away layers of blank wrapping paper, crumpling them in my hands as my mind wrapped around my father leaving me a final gift. I pulled away the last layer of paper and saw a glint of sunlight reflect off the round diamond set inside a silver horseshoe that sat on a blue sapphire—my father's ring from Super Bowl V. The ring's rectangular top bore in relief the words *Baltimore Colts* on one side, *World Champions* on the other. One side of the ring had the outline of a Super Bowl trophy positioned between the numbers *19* and *70*, the year he won it. And on the other side of the ring, etched in yellow gold, above the side profile of a Colts helmet, was the gift my father had given me, the gift of a good name. Sandusky.

— Chapter Twelve —

THE MEANING OF A NAME

November 2011

When I returned home in the early morning hours after the Ravens' win in Pittsburgh on Monday Night Football, I felt the tug of curiosity to check my Twitter feed and see whether the emerging digital storm on social media had calmed down over the name confusion between Jerry Sandusky and Gerry Sandusky. It shocked me how much misplaced hatred people could condense into 140 characters. Hate messages sloshed into my Twitter account, spilling and splashing over any boundaries of fairness and good taste. Some accused me of rape. Some presumed the coach arrested was my father. Most mentions of my name on Twitter came attached to invitations to spend eternity in hell. Unable to sleep, I sat at my desk in the loft above our master bedroom and began tapping on the keyboard of my laptop, sending the first of what would become thousands of replies: "You have the wrong guy. I'm Gerry with a G, no relation to the Penn State guy."

Before long I felt under siege.

Dozens of messages a day streamed into my account, nearly all of them laced with venom:

"I hope you get raped in prison."

"How could you do that to all of those boys?"

"You are a sicko."

"You're a pervert!"

"Stay away from my children!"

"You filthy son of a [bleep]."

Within a few days the traffic on my Twitter account grew to hundreds of messages a day, most with a negative tone. I changed the bio on my Twitter account to read, "I am Gerry with a G. Baltimore sportscaster. No relation to the former Penn State coach." Still, people couldn't seem to pick up on the obvious difference that the coach arrested and charged as a pedophile spells his first name with a J, and I spell mine with a G. One person accused me of guilt by association. Apparently the seventh and tenth letters of the alphabet are conspirators.

Then the second wave arrived—the endless advice to change my name. It came dressed in the finery of well wishes, but it grated on me even more deeply than the haters, whom I could dismiss as fools.

This tweet made my heart plunge with the realization of how many people now equated my name with evil: "Have you considered changing your name slightly? Maybe Gerry Hitler or Gerry Bin Laden?" More followed: "You're a monster. You're a sick sick monster. I hope you burn in hell for what u did to those children."

Each night at work I looked across the expanse of the newsroom at WBAL-TV, a cavernous rectangular room with a twenty-foot-tall ceiling covered with a grid of metal bars that held TV lights. Rows of desks filled the room. Each desk belonged to a coworker—an anchor, reporter, or producer—and gave a glimpse into that storyteller's life: photos of a wedding, riding waves at the ocean, cycling with their children, a graduate's smile beneath a mortar board, a stack of outdated video tapes, a plastic recycling bin with old script paper spilling over the sides, a dog-eared dictionary, manila file folders spread out like playing cards in Texas hold 'em. Every night one of those colleagues, and sometimes several of them, worked on a Jerry Sandusky story. I could always tell which ones. When I walked by a desk, if I made eye contact with someone who quickly looked away or mumbled an apology, I knew—their turn tonight. The industry I worked in compounded my problem with seemingly endless coverage of the Joe Paterno–Jerry Sandusky–Penn State scandal. Every day brought a new legal motion, a new witness, another press conference, with each one attached to a name that most of America now equated with a monster.

NBC news anchor Brian Williams. Diane Sawyer on ABC. Scott Pelley on CBS. CNN, FOX, MSNBC, ESPN—every news outlet in America had a nightly story on the mushrooming fallout from the Jerry Sandusky scandal. If you didn't look at the TV but just listened, you couldn't tell any difference between Jerry Sandusky and Gerry Sandusky. They sound the same. Spelling my first name with a G instead of a J gave me only a slim shield in a world angry—and for good reason—at a man alleged to have committed heinous crimes, a man whose name eroded my own.

Two weeks after the story first broke, Lee Ann and I lay in bed watching *Saturday Night Live* when we saw the first of what would become many Jerry Sandusky parodies. Lee Ann turned off the TV, rolled over, folded herself in my arms, and cried. This wasn't going to go away for a long time. And it was tearing up my family.

The next day I gathered Lee Ann, Katy, and Zack for a family meeting in our loft. It's our retreat, where we tune out the world, a world that had become decidedly uglier with each mention of our family name.

Katy and Zack looked bewildered. Zack's mouth hung slightly open, ready to say something but not sure when to begin. Katy's nostrils flared, anger pulsing across her soft skin. They heard the bad jokes and snarky comments at school, and they had the street fighter's stare I remembered having after Super Bowl III when I heard kids in school ridicule my father for the Colts' loss to the Jets. It's the stare that begs someone to say something negative directly to you—an insult, an expletive, a rude remark—so you can lash out and unload your pent-up anger. No one wants to see his father attacked unfairly without a chance to fight back. A day after I got into a fight at recess with a kid who called my father a loser, the biggest loser ever in the NFL, my father let Joe get out of the car first when he dropped us off at school. He put his hand on my shoulder. "I want to have a little talk with you," he said. He didn't use the word *conversation*. I understood the implication: he would talk; I would listen.

"I know what happened yesterday," he began. I felt a flutter of panic in my stomach, the precursor to punishment. "And I understand why you punched that kid. It probably felt good," he said, adding a smile that I didn't expect. "But you can't do it again." He pulled his eyebrows down into a stern look. "You can't punch your way out of stupid people saying stupid things. There's a lot of stupid in this world, and if you try to fight it, you're the only one who will wind up looking bad. I'll be fine and so will you. But you have to learn to stand tall."

"But Dad," I began to protest, but he cut me off.

"No buts. Real strength comes from deep inside," he tapped his sternum with his index finger. "You hold on to that strength until the stupid goes away. No matter how long it takes."

His look penetrated deeper than my eyes, which I blinked furiously, holding back tears. His words and his stare soaked into my skin, my bones, my marrow, my future.

Now, all these years later, I understood what my father had told me. And I understood what we had to do as a family.

It was my turn to look my children in the eyes.

Katy, now a beautiful young woman in college, with long brown hair, her grandmother's delicate hands, a fashion model's high cheekbones, gave me a look with her brown eyes that needed no words to explain. She wanted to attack anyone, everyone who had spoken poorly about me, about us. Zack, a high school junior with a warm smile and a wiry frame he had only begun growing into, had a more bewildered look. The small, pie-shaped slice of blue in his left eye that usually made his otherwise brown eyes sparkle seemed to spin now, a wobbling top. Lee Ann, with her shoulder-length brown hair pulled back, had the outline of dark bags beneath her eyes from a sleepless night. Her lower lip pouted, quivered, a thread-thin teeterboard between anger and tears.

"You can all stop worrying about me," I told them. "I've been through far worse. My job is to protect you," I said. "I don't need you to agree with me, but I do need you to trust me. A lighthouse doesn't fight a storm. It stands tall in a storm. And that's what we're going to do. Each of us. No matter what people say to us or about us, no matter what you hear people say about me or to me, we aren't going to react."

I held up my hand to rebuff Katy's first protest before she had let the first word escape from her lips.

"It will take a while, maybe a long while, but in time how we handle this will define us as a family. That doesn't mean you won't want to scream, throw something, cry, or wish you could punch someone about the injustice. I know that. We all feel that. So we'll cry together. We'll scream together. We'll do it here, but not out there. I want you to be a lighthouse."

I didn't know whether I was making the right decision as to how to approach this, and I could tell from the simmering looks in front of me that my wife and children thought of inaction as weakness. The corners of Zack's eyes seemed to droop. The corners of Lee Ann's lips twitched. Katy shook her head slowly, side to side. They all wanted to hear something different from me, something more aggressive. The high road sounded lonely and long.

I knew my kids and my wife would never hear a word I ever said again if I didn't live up to the standard I had asked them to meet. The next several months gave me plenty of opportunities to find out whether I could.

The week before Christmas, while Zack and I shopped at a Best Buy near our house, a man in his forties, wearing a baseball cap, a Penn State sweatshirt, and blue jeans and walking next to his wife and two young daughters, came up to me while Zack and I perused the camera aisle. The man said loudly, "Hey, I didn't think they let rapists out of jail to do their Christmas shopping." He started to laugh. Zack looked at me, and I stared at the man without blinking, a blank look that reflected the ignorance of his comment. The man's wife took his hand and backed the family away, mumbling an apology.

Zack looked at me and smiled. He had begun to understand stillness came from strength, not weakness.

Not five minutes later, as Zack and I walked toward the checkout counter, an older man in his seventies with a scraggly beard and tobacco-stained mustache reached out and grabbed my arm as we walked past. He had craggy skin and a husky voice that suggested a familiarity with whiskey. I was used to these types of encounters. When you work on television, people feel like they know you and can strike up conversations with you in public.

"That your boy?" the old man asked.

I nodded.

"Does he know about all the bad things you did to all those other boys?"

Again, I returned a blank stare uninterrupted by a blink, pushing as far to the basement of my belly my desire to reach out and clutch the man's throat and demand an apology.

Then I continued on my walk to the front of the store, feeling anger fill my breath, burning hot gas in my lungs. As much as I wanted to, I couldn't make anyone feel better about our name by punching an old man in a store, even one too stupid to think his words didn't lance my patience or my son's pride. The only person I could conquer was myself. The only enemy I could defeat was my anger.

I had asked my family to be a lighthouse, but I hadn't told them how long the storm would last. I didn't know. But I did know it would change every one of us.

Deadspin called. So did *Esquire*. The NFL Network. *The Baltimore Sun*. The *Dallas Morning News*. Radio stations from Portland, Maine, to San Diego, California, called. They all wanted to know what it felt like to have so much of the country confuse me with an accused pedophile, to see a Jerry Sandusky story every night on national news broadcasts, to receive more hate mail than junk mail.

It felt unfair. I felt helpless. It felt like someone had stolen my name, my family's good name.

I had asked my wife and children to believe me, to believe that standing tall in the face of hatred and ignorance would work. I knew that, like me, every day they faced the "Sandusky stare," the slightly wide-eyed look from people at the grocery store, the dry cleaners, the school cafeteria, the practice field, the look that lingered a heartbeat too long and revealed their insatiable desire to know whether we were related to the former coach from Penn State who had outraged a nation with his violation of boys.

At night, when I returned home from work after anchoring the sportscast in the eleven o'clock news, I retreated to the loft, grateful for a part of the day where no one could see me stare into the darkness or hear doubt ringing in my thoughts as I wondered whether I had put my family on the right path, whether there was a right path. I didn't know anyone who had gone through something like this, and I had to pretend that I knew how to handle it, that I could handle it.

Even what had started to look like a great football season for the Ravens offered no relief from the challenge of letting the storm pass over.

After winning their division and earning a week off to start the post-season, the Ravens beat Houston in the divisional round of the playoffs and advanced to the AFC Championship game in Foxboro, Massachusetts, against the New England Patriots. By the time kickoff arrived midafternoon, an icy wind swirling through Foxboro's Gillette Stadium had driven the wind chill into the low twenties.

By that point in the season I had grown used to facing a barrage of mean-spirited comments from fans in other team's stadiums. The radio broadcast booth in most stadiums has an open rectangular front that looks out on the field from near the forty-yard line. Many of the booths, including the one in Foxboro, sit between the lower and upper decks, barely a head above the nearest row of fans, whose seats butt up against the bottom of the booth. Fans heckle visiting broadcasters as much as visiting players, and as the Jerry Sandusky story grew, more and more fans found out my name too. Patriots fans seated near our broadcast booth made a point of calling out my name and attaching comments as cold as the weather:

"Hey rapist, watcha doin outta prison?"

"Wicked thing ya done to all them kids."

"First you're gonna lose. Then you're going to hell."

I avoided eye contact and held my attention on the field.

My broadcast partners, Stan White and Qadry Ismail, both played in the NFL. Stan with the Colts in the seventies, Qadry with the Ravens during their first Super Bowl run in the 2000 season. They had watched me endure weekly target practice from haters. A drunken Patriots fan, with cheeks illuminated by both the cold and something distilled, stood beneath our booth and shouted, "Sandusky, why don't you change your name? That's a bad name. Guess that makes you a bad man."

Stan, who played linebacker in the NFL for eleven years, yanked off his headset, threw it on the counter in front of him, turned off his microphone, and pointed at the Patriots fan, shouting, "Shut up. Say one more word and I will come down there and kick your ass. Am I clear?"

The flush of red in the heckling fan's face vanished before he turned and melded back into the crowd, glancing over his shoulder to make sure Stan didn't follow him.

Qadry did.

He walked out of the broadcast booth, down to the stands, and let security know that either they start keeping fans away from our booth or else he and Stan would.

Lee Ann, Zack, and Katy made the trip to Foxboro. Lee Ann wanted a Ravens trip to the Super Bowl to become a family experience, the same hope most Ravens fans had.

Before every game Katy had a tradition of sending me the same message just before kickoff: "Broadcast like a champion." Today she added one more line: "Make Pop-Pop proud."

By the third quarter, with the Ravens leading the Patriots, New England fans in front of us took on a mood that matched the oyster shell–colored clouds above the stadium. Our broadcast booth and my name had slipped from their attention.

A text from Zack read, "Ravens might do this!"

A Tom Brady touchdown midway through the fourth quarter put New England back in front, but the Ravens rallied late in the game, putting together a ten-play drive with time winding down.

With less than a minute in the game to play and the Ravens trailing by three points, a pass from Ravens quarterback Joe Flacco to receiver Anquan Boldin put the ball at the Patriots fourteen-yard line, easily within field goal range to tie it and with enough time left to win the game.

On the next play Flacco dropped back to pass. I looked down from the broadcast booth and carried listeners through the moment: "Twenty-nine seconds left. Ravens at the threshold of a trip to the Super Bowl. Flacco to throw. Looks right. Pumps," I said, knowing the heart and hope of every Ravens fan wrapped around the play as tightly as I clutched the Sharpie pen in my right hand.

"Throws. End zone!"

Adrenaline pulsed through me, my heart outpacing the rhythm of each second ticking off the game clock. The sting of cold weather had disappeared. A trip to the Super Bowl rode on the outcome of the play.

Indianapolis hosted the Super Bowl. Indy—the town the Baltimore Colts had moved to in the middle of the night three decades before, eviscerating every football fan in Baltimore and leaving most of Maryland with a weekly void on Sundays in the fall until the Ravens arrived thirteen years later. Indianapolis, long a twist of agony to Baltimore football fans, could now become a destination, a trip only fourteen yards and twenty-eight seconds away.

The ball traveled on the slightest arc toward the end zone along the near sideline.

"Caught. Touchdown! Lee Evans!" I shouted. My hands flew up in the air, mirroring an official's signal for a touchdown. Then the mirror broke. "No. He can't hang on. Stirling Martin stripped away the ball before Evans could get a second foot down in the end zone."

The broadest emotional spectrum had played out to the soundtrack of my voice, tantalizing to torture, a rise to euphoria, a crash to disappointment.

After another incompletion, the Ravens had to settle for a field goal attempt to tie the game to send it to overtime. The Ravens' kicker, Billy Cundiff, who had gone to the Pro Bowl the year before, ran onto the field for a thirty-two-yard field goal attempt, a kick so easy I had begun reminding listeners of the new overtime rules in the NFL.

My phone vibrated with a text from Zack: "We'll win this in O.T."

Then came the final curve in a difficult year. With fifteen seconds left, Cundiff, who hadn't missed a field goal in the fourth quarter in the previous two years, hooked his kick. It sailed wide left. No good. The miss sent the Patriots to the Super Bowl.

A minute after thinking I would spend the next two weeks preparing for a Super Bowl broadcast in Indianapolis, I felt the air rush from my lungs while a heaviness plunged from my chest to my stomach to my legs and to my feet, the leaden weight of unrealized dreams. Words that formed themselves leapt from my lips into the microphone, my mind numb. Despair stretched from the Ravens sideline below in the direction of the locker room beneath the stadium on the far side of the field as players walked as mechanically as robots across the field, motion drained of emotion. On the TV monitor in front of me the screen captured Ravens running back Ray Rice's expression, eyes blank, mouth open, the stare of a man robbed of his tomorrow.

Patriots fans, who had grown quiet on the Ravens' final drive of the game, surged back to life. Thousands dressed in blue Patriots down jackets, player jerseys, and wool caps streamed by our broadcast booth, dancing, hugging, yelling on their way out of the stadium. Several took a last opportunity to remind me of the burden my name had become:

"Good luck in prison this off-season."

"I hope somebody rapes you this time."

"Last game you get to go to for the next twenty years to life."

Stan had gone to the locker room to do interviews. Qadry pulled off his headset, ready to wade into the tide that fomented in front of us, but

I put my hand on his shoulder and shook my head: *Let it go*. The past few months had taught me the only fight that matters is within.

I thought of my father and what I saw of him from a distance through my binoculars in the moments after Super Bowl III, the forward tilt of his head, the forty-five-degree angle of his stare toward the ground, the slope of his usually square shoulders, all from the weight of disappointment that engulfed him. I hoped my wife and children now had their binoculars trained on someone other than me, because I suspected each of those physical traits that poured through my binoculars into my memory forty-two years earlier had returned, this time to my body, not my eyes.

During a commercial break I peeled off my headset and looked at a text message from Zack: "Sorry Dad. A Super Bowl trip would've made up for this year."

The day and the season had come to an end I knew too well: disappointment that bridged two generations, a family tradition I had hoped not to pass along.

Over the next six months the legal process and maneuvers in the Jerry Sandusky case kept the story in the national news nearly every day. By the June start of the trial I couldn't turn on a TV, go online, or listen to a radio newscast without seeing or hearing the name that sounded identical to mine. But unlike eight months earlier, when news of criminal acts first intersected with what sounded like my name, time had given me a perspective and a power from not screaming "unfair" at everyone who did a double-take when they heard my name. Three days after a jury convicted Jerry Sandusky on twenty-five felonies and twenty misdemeanors, I wrote a blog outlining insights I had gleaned from the bizarre threat to my name. In a sense I transcribed it as much as I wrote it. Sometimes words pass through you and your fingertips catch them. Mine did. After I finished typing them on my laptop I reread what had, in a blur, moved from my thoughts to my computer screen. It struck me that most of what I saw in front of me were lessons I had learned from my father, a few from my mother too, lessons they had taught me with their lives, not words.

- Don't run; don't hide. You can't.
- Like it or not, you now have a platform. Use it for good.
- Don't try to fight a tidal wave. Ride it. Your first task is to survive.
- Don't react to ignorance, hatred, or meanness.
- Saying "Thank you" always has more power than saying "%$# you."
- Maintain your poise.
- Take the high road. If nothing else, you will show some people that a high road exists.
- You can't change or control the world before you change and control yourself. Start with yourself.
- Pray for the people who have suffered more than you. Their wounds are deeper than yours, and your prayers can help them.
- Remember, it's temporary. No one lives forever on this planet, so his or her problems—and yours—have a shelf life too.
- When it's appropriate, laugh. Everyone's laughing behind your back; you might as well have a little fun too.
- Be a winner, not a whiner. Don't waste time whining about "why me?" The world has enough whiners. It never has enough winners.
- Learn and draw strength from the examples of others. Gandhi, Alfred Nobel, Helen Keller, Martin Luther King Jr., andcountless others all stood up to injustice, misfortune, or bad circumstances and changed the world for the better. You can too.
- Hating is always about the haters. It's not about you.
- Lean on your own life experience. I have thought of Joe often over the past year and smiled, thinking I've survived one of the worst things life could throw at me, and I did it one day at a time without having all the answers. It also reminded me that I didn't need all the answers to handle this situation too.

- Talk to your kids often. They hurt too, and they hurt for you. Show them you're okay and you'll help them be okay too.
- Never fight fire with fire. No stupid, ignorant, mean-spirited, or hate-filled person ever chose to change because someone called him stupid, ignorant, mean spirited, or hate-filled.
- Remember that those who came before you left you with a good name. Commit to doing the same for those who will come after you.

The following season the Baltimore Ravens did make it to the Super Bowl, Super Bowl XLVII in New Orleans. Several hours before the game I did an interview with Rich Eisen beneath the bright lights of the NFL Network's temporary studio on the Ravens sideline, a five-minute segment. Not once did the topic of my name work its way into the conversation. I had weathered the storm. So had my wife, my daughter, and my son.

All three of them had come to the Super Dome for the game, for the shared experience, come what may. When they arrived in the stadium the Ravens' season highlights played on the scoreboard with my touchdown calls reverberating beneath the golden roof of the Super Dome.

Zack sent me a text: "Coolest thing ever."

Katy sent me her usual pregame text: "Broadcast like a champion." This time she added, "You've already made Pop-Pop proud. I love you."

In the final few moments leading up to the start of our broadcast I soaked up the energy that percolated all around me. Fans dressed in purple Ravens jerseys and red San Francisco 49ers jerseys. Players jogging in the end zone. Coaches shaking hands at midfield. CBS, ESPN, NFL Network—all broadcasting from field-level studios, complete with bright lights, big anchor desks, and jib cameras, the kind that work on a radial arm and give sweeping panoramic shots of the field and beg for an orchestral musical score to accompany them.

I wanted to retreat, to gather my thoughts before I opened my microphone and chased the football with my words for the next three and a half hours. I walked to the men's room across the hallway and stepped into a stall, the only private, quiet space available. And I listened. At first I heard only my breathing—a little shallow, filled with tension. After a minute or two my breathing slowed, and I heard what I sought: the distant echo of my father's voice, his smile wrapped around it. I didn't hear it with my ears. I heard it the way I heard my father as a boy, a teenager, a young man. I heard it with my eyes, my heart, my bones. A sensation brushed across the hair on my forearms and the back of my neck, a feeling, a knowing, a presence. Somewhere across the gulf that separates the living and the dead, a gulf that words don't traverse but emotions do, I could hear my father remember the magic of Sundays, the day that had shaped his life and mine. He remembered what made them special.

Enjoy today. Really enjoy it.

What felt like the heft of his hand on my shoulder accompanied me as I walked back toward the broadcast booth. My producer, his face flushed, stood at the door of the booth, screaming, "We're on in less than thirty seconds. Where have you been?"

I didn't answer him. I had made a trip all men hope to make, the journey to know my father. I walked to the front of the broadcast booth and looked out over the packed Super Dome. The Super Bowl logo emblazoned in the middle of the field, one end zone painted purple with the word *Ravens* written in white, the other painted red with *49ers* also in white. I turned on my microphone, and I smiled. I knew that no matter what happened for the rest of the evening, I would remember it forever. I looked out over the purple and red sea of fans and felt a tide of contentment fill me.

Along with sharing this day with listeners on the radio, I would share it with my wife, son, and daughter. Long after this game no longer stood at the front of the country's attention, long after Lee Ann and I had become memories ourselves, Katy and Zack would hold on to the shared experience. We all would, from different perspectives. A day, a moment destined to fade into the archives of websites would remain alive in each of us. Just as I prepared to say my first words I saw the memory of my father, younger than I was now, walking onto the field at his first Super Bowl, and I smiled, realizing there are no forgotten Sundays.

∾⤬∾

Four months later, following the ceremony at the Ravens' team facility to celebrate their Super Bowl win and to hand out Super Bowl rings, I returned home, and after Lee Ann, Katy, and Zack had gone to bed, I walked up to the loft, the room where eighteen months before I had asked them to each find the courage to be a lighthouse, an unmovable force in a storm, a strength I didn't know whether I had, much less had the right to ask them to rise to. But it was a strength I had seen before, a strength I knew existed.

I put my Super Bowl ring on a bookshelf next to my father's ring. Mine sat in a black onyx box with a Ravens logo etched into the top, his on a blue satin cushion in a Plexiglas case. Our family name stared back at me, raised in yellow gold on his ring, white gold on mine, and I realized I never fully knew the man who gave me his name until I thought he was gone, only to discover he never completely left me. He became part of me, a part that defines more than the mix of brown and gray in my hair, the lines that run through my palms like threads on a football, the angles and curves of my profile. He remains a part that lives in a canyon of my soul and whispers in moments when I think I stand alone, moments drenched with doubt when I crave the guidance of a map, the assurance of directions. And the whisper assures me that I do have them. I've had them all along. It's the map my father shared at my birth and left me at his death. It's the map of a single word, the map of our name.